Inclusive Character Analysis

Inclusive Character Analysis foregrounds representations of race, gender, class, ability, and sexual orientation by blending script analysis with a variety of critical theories in order to create a more inclusive performance practice for the classroom and the stage.

This book merges a traditional Stanislavski-based script analysis with multiple theoretical frameworks, such as gender theory, standpoint theory, and critical race theory, to give students in early level theatre courses foundational skills for analyzing a play, while also introducing them to contemporary thought about race, gender, and identity.

Inclusive Character Analysis is a valuable resource for beginning acting courses, script analysis courses, the directing classroom, early design curriculum, dramaturgical explorations, the playwriting classroom, and introduction to performance studies classes. Additionally, the book offers a reader-style background on theoretical frames for performance faculty and practitioners who may need assistance to integrate non-performance centered theory into their classrooms.

Jennifer Thomas is an Associate Professor of Performance and Chair of Performance and Communication Arts Department at St. Lawrence University, where she teaches courses in theatre history, theory, and literature. Working at the intersection of theory and practice, Thomas's work has explored aging and old age, ethnography and musical theatre, and higher education pedagogy and practices in and out of the theatre. Her creative scholarship has been seen in Washington, Oregon, North Dakota, Connecticut, and Wisconsin.

Robert J. Vrtis is an Associate Professor of Theatre at Luther College. He teaches classes in acting, contemporary theatre, and directing practices. At Luther College, he works to empower student voices through service on the Council for Equity and Inclusion.

Inclusive Character Analysis

Putting Theory into Practice for the 21st Century Theatre Classroom

Jennifer Thomas and
Robert J. Vrtis

Routledge
Taylor & Francis Group

NEW YORK AND LONDON

First published 2021
by Routledge
52 Vanderbilt Avenue, New York, NY 10017

and by Routledge
2 Park Square, Milton Park, Abingdon, Oxon, OX14 4RN

Routledge is an imprint of the Taylor & Francis Group, an informa business

© 2021 Taylor & Francis

The right of Jennifer Thomas and Robert J. Vrtis to be identified as authors of this work has been asserted by them in accordance with sections 77 and 78 of the Copyright, Designs and Patents Act 1988.

All rights reserved. No part of this book may be reprinted or reproduced or utilised in any form or by any electronic, mechanical, or other means, now known or hereafter invented, including photocopying and recording, or in any information storage or retrieval system, without permission in writing from the publishers.

Trademark notice: Product or corporate names may be trademarks or registered trademarks, and are used only for identification and explanation without intent to infringe.

Library of Congress Cataloging-in-Publication Data
Names: Thomas, Jennifer (College teacher), author. | Vrtis, Robert J., author.
Title: Inclusive character analysis : putting theory into practice for the 21st century theatre classroom / Jennifer Thomas and Robert J. Vrtis.
Description: New York : Routledge, 2021. | Includes bibliographical references and index.
Identifiers: LCCN 2020033313 (print) | LCCN 2020033314 (ebook) | ISBN 9780367358426 (hardback) | ISBN 9780367358327 (paperback) | ISBN 9780429342226 (ebook)
Subjects: LCSH: Acting--Study and teaching. | Drama--Explication. | Theater--Production and direction.
Classification: LCC PN2075 .T56 2021 (print) | LCC PN2075 (ebook) | DDC 792.028--dc23
LC record available at https://lccn.loc.gov/2020033313
LC ebook record available at https://lccn.loc.gov/2020033314

ISBN: 978-0-367-35842-6 (hbk)
ISBN: 978-0-367-35832-7 (pbk)
ISBN: 978-0-429-34222-6 (ebk)

Typeset in Sabon
by KnowledgeWorks Global Ltd.

Contents

	Acknowledgements	vi
	Introduction	1
1	Reading the Language of the Play	11
2	Standpoint Theory and If	33
3	Place Theory and Given Circumstances	60
4	Gender Theory and Relationships	84
5	Class Privilege and Desire	108
6	Critical Race Theory and Beats	131
7	Disability Studies and Internal/External Adjustments	161
	Conclusion: Wrapping It Up	176
	Index	179

Acknowledgements

This book rests on the hard work of many who have been cited within and whose work we want to urge readers toward. We also want to acknowledge several people for their provocations, insights, support, and kindness.

Thank you to Stacey Walker at Routledge, who caught an early morning session at ATHE and saw a spark of this book. Thank you also to Lucia Accorsi, whose timelines were put to the test due to illnesses, pandemics, global moves and general malaise due to a world on fire.

Dr. Barbara Love's Social Justice Pedagogy workshop helped give focus early in this process, as well as a sense of urgency that proved to be a much needed push. Lisa Scott, Sean Burke, Anna Sorenson, Kate Elliott, Jessica Sierk, Christine Doran, Stephen Barnard, Allison Rowland, Emily Hamilton-Honey, and David Thompson provided direction to resources that helped shape the writing throughout this process and sharpened our attention to specific theory and content. Jane Hawley is an inspiration for always thinking about, including all bodies in the dance. Thank you to Richard Merritt for insight and encouragement at the dry erase board phase. A shout out to Megan Orcholski for always reminding us to clarify language and not fear making mistakes…for there is learning in that experience. Thank you to Stephen Rupsch for his friendship, mentorship and brainstorming during this project. And a very special thank you to our graduate school mentor, Dr. John Schmor, who taught us to move toward our fears and resistances. We are both better educators and humans because of you.

Our students have been instrumental in setting us on this course. Some provided small pushes and redirections, while others reminded us that we can do better, and a few offered direct assistance on the work itself. These students are too numerous to call out individually, but a few certainly deserve a mention. We would like to express our thanks to Michael Ehrecke, Maggie Sulentic, Tim Komatsu, Gillian Constable, Ursula Martin, Emily Brisson, Lewinski Lopez, Sara Christensen, Brian Uceta, Hamidou Sylla, Madeline Geier, Eva Gemlo, Elaena Hoekstra, Laila Sahir, Anna Becker, and Clare Rolinger. Thank you to the students we have learned from in the classrooms of the University of Oregon, Concordia College, Luther College, and St. Lawrence University. Never let up and keep pushing us to grow and learn alongside you.

Special thanks to the powerhouse contributions of our partners, Christina Vrtis and Danny Thomas. Without their push and support…this project wouldn't have made it to the finish line.

Introduction

The Necessity of this Project: A Note of Introduction from Jennifer

Several years ago, a student approached me in a beginning acting classroom and identified themselves as non-binary with a request for they/them pronouns. This was not my first encounter with a non-binary student; however, it was my first encounter with a non-binary student in an acting classroom. I wish I could say that I handled the conversation perfectly, that I had easily handled script choices and character analyses options efficiently and reflectively. But mostly, I asked some awkward questions to which the student responded in the kindest and most learning-centered way and I bumbled my way forward that semester failing and learning over and over. It was during this repetition of failing and learning that I realized that the theatre claims to be a space of inclusivity, but our actor training and analysis work does not reflect that inclusivity. There is a presumption of whiteness, able-bodiedness, an over-reliance on binaries, and other dominant narratives pervading how we discuss characters and their worlds.

I have been drawn to intersections of theory and practice in my work as a student, scholar, educator, and artist. As a first-generation college student, I have always been drawn to how people know what they know. In my undergraduate education, I was baffled by how folks around me understood higher education. It didn't even dawn on me that being a professor was a career that I could have. I had no idea how people even got to be professors. In my first graduate theory class, I remember sobbing over my homework because the words in my textbook weren't in my dictionary (this was pre-internet) and I didn't understand how I was supposed to learn the theory if I couldn't even figure out what a word meant.

I offer up these experiences from my past to share my vulnerabilities. The work we ask you to do in this book will create feelings of discomfort and resistance and vulnerability. It is the nature of the work. Opening the space to diverse perspectives and experiences can be unsettling and that is exactly why we should do it. In fact, putting this book out in the public sphere is an act of vulnerability as the ideas in this book, the theory and social constructions of identity, are ever-shifting and changing. By the time this book is in your hands, some of the language and conversations will have moved on or completely changed focus. And that is ok. What is important is that we are engaging publicly in the vulnerable work of including social and cultural positions not always engaged with in lives of our characters.

My interest in theory, and perhaps more importantly accessible theory, has been key in my own academic classrooms as a professor and on stage as a theatre artist. Where can gender theory, queer theory, fat studies, critical race theory, and so many others come into the daily conversation of my classroom and rehearsals? How can these theories and conversations impact script and character analysis?

By moving away from hegemonic standards in our character analyses, we can manifest, for ourselves and our students, a diverse and inclusive understanding and interpretation of characters. Examining a character's identity is a way of not only teaching analysis but also exposing students to an understanding of identity that translates to the world beyond the theatre classroom. The theatre classroom can become a practice ground for learning about and undertaking conversations surrounding diversity, privilege, and inclusion, for example. Using our characters as a less-personal way to engage in conversations that require vulnerability and openness is a great stepping stone to moving these practices and understanding to ourselves and the world around us.

An intersectional and interdisciplinary approach drives this book and largely stems from the following statement by Jill Dolan, feminist theatre scholar, in "Geographies of Learning: Theatre Studies, Performance, and the 'Performative'." Dolan writes, "I intend to argue here for the retention of theatre studies as a disciplinary 'home' deeply influenced by interdisciplinary methods, one made less coherent and less safe (even dangerous) by its determined inclusion of other(ed) geographies, other(ed) desires, and bodies othered by what hegemony has refused to allow seen" (421). Dolan is calling for an artform that is more capacious and responsive to identities that have not been foregrounded in the theatre or our most familiar systems of actor training. These "othered" identities belong in the theatre as theatre artists and as characters. The approach offered in this book is an attempt to move away from assumed and exclusionary practices by using interdisciplinarity and critical theory to center the othered in theatre practice.

Our Particular Points of View: A Note of Introduction from Robert

It'd be difficult for me to pinpoint where this book came from, and what exactly began it. Instead, when I think of how Jen and I began to ask how we could frame a more inclusive character analysis, I think of conversations about our work with students. More precisely for me, working mostly with young actors in a studio setting, how well I was justified in claiming that my class was a welcoming and inclusive space. A safe place to express yourself, whoever you are. A place where you saw yourself reflected in the curriculum.

Early on, we agreed that those of us who teach theatre may too readily give ourselves undeserved credit for inclusion of diverse voices, for being part of an art form where all are made to feel valued and welcome. Over and over, the people I have met in theatre express some form of this as a personal and artistic value, an ideal of this wonderful and deeply empathetic art. But, I also know that I have fallen short of these ideals in my studio or in rehearsals, making someone feel marginalized. I can also assume that for the shortfalls I am conscious of and remember, there are undoubtedly moments I missed entirely with some unconscious assumption or comment.

As we returned again and again to this self-analysis, I felt the slow emergence of assumptions I've held that urgently needed to be questioned. Is my studio open and welcoming to diverse perspectives? Does it honor and respect people from all backgrounds and their unique identities? Is it inclusive? Do I even have the tools to make an inclusive space? This book is, in part, the result of that questioning. It can't do all the work, but I believe it is a significant step toward meeting the ideals of a more inclusive theatre.

While working on this text, I've struggled over whether I am the best person to write it at all. In order to be upfront with you from the beginning, I will say that I identify as a straight, white, cisgender male. My writing partner on this text is a straight, white, cisgender female. Physically and neurologically, I would fall into what my culture would typically deem "normal." I want to, therefore, acknowledge that as I write, trying to create a more inclusive way to approach character analysis, I necessarily write from a position of privilege. For that reason, I want to use this introduction to be clear about what I hope I can do from that position, and stress what I am not going to try to do.

In this book, we'll often write about a character's *particular point of view*—the very specific vantage point from which they experience their world. That particular point of view is unique to them because it is constructed by the specific circumstances in which they live, all the components of their identity, and the experiences that have led them to this point. I too have a particular point of view, as I suggested a moment ago. That is a particular point of view that I can never fully leave behind, however much I might try to see the world through another's eyes.

Because I can never fully leave this particular point of view behind, it would be foolish of me to try to tell someone else their own experience to them. Even as I write to encourage actors to inhabit a point of view other than their own, I know there are limits to this possibility. So, I will say that this text is not intended to dictate your experience of the world to you. Rather, I want to give you tools that I think will help you foster the kind of deep empathy that can help you come close to experiencing a character's world. At the same time, I hope the construction of this book will make space for actors whose particular point of view is different from my own, and who may not always see their experiences reflected in texts of this kind, to use those tools.

Character Analysis and An Introduction to the Exercises

The character analysis we encourage in this book should help you bring the text of a play to life by creating a full fictional life for the people in that text. It is meant to help you understand a play through those people who enact its story. From there, these characters may be performed by you, their world designed by you, or you may direct the performance of their story on the stage.

However you use this book, you will be creating a fantasy world that is founded on the text of a play or growing out of it. There is a tremendous amount of room for your own creativity in this process, but you should always be sure of that foundation and avoid creating something that the foundation will not support. This could be as simple as realizing that you've imagined a summer day outside and suddenly realizing that another character came in stomping snow off their boots or commented that they almost slipped on a patch of ice. It could also be a significant difference between the way you envision a character's background and what you subsequently learn from the text about their history. If the text of the play directly contradicts the world of the play that you are creating for yourself, you'll need to reconcile that schism in a way that respects the text.

Chapter by chapter, we'll explore different elements of character analysis, each helping to establish some component of a character's being. Because the playwright's words are the entryway into the world of the play, in Chapter 1 we will start by investigating the language and structure of the play. Chapter 2 will begin the process of understanding the character's point of view and how we begin to imagine ourselves into their lives. With this perspective created, Chapter 3 moves into the world of given circustances (or facts established by the play), weaving perspectives and circumstances together.

Once your character's world is largely established in these initial chapters, we will begin to determine the way they navigate their world. One of the most important ways that a character connects to their world is through the other people who populate it. In Chapter 4, we will specifically focus on the way a character relates to other people. What are the relationships they form? What are these relationships based on? What roles do they play and when do those roles change? We've also used this chapter to give special attention a character's experience of gender, sex, and sexuality.

Chapter 5 focuses on the forces that drive a character through the story of a play—desires, wants, and needs. We also take the opportunity to complicate identity by considering the implications of class and class privilege on a character's life. We can see a character's identity is as complex as our own by acknowledging that we move through the world with multiple aspects of identity that intersect within our particular point of view.

Characters must take action in order to get what they want, to satisfy their needs, or to otherwise realize their desires. In Chapter 6, we will consider what actions a character will attempt in pursuit of their goals. This chapter also opens up a discussion on race with a particular consideration for the way one's actions may be shaped by social expectations, assumptions, and biases in the broader culture around them.

In Chapter 7, we acknowledge that inhabiting a character may require the actor to make physical adjustments or consider how a character's mind may operate differently than their own. This chapter suggests we take time to make an inventory of the operations of our body and mind, considering that the way we move through or process the world we perceive is not universal.

Brought together, these elements compose a character in all their complexity—their history, their identity, their hopes, their ideals, and all that which makes them fully human. The more detail that we can establish about a character the more vivid and credible their reality becomes to us and to an audience. In that sense, the concepts introduced in each chapter will add more dimension and definition to that world, layer by layer.

Throughout this text, we've devised exercises that are intended to deepen your understanding of a given concept while you create a richly detailed character based on the text of a play. Often, the exercises are generated under the assumption that you have been assigned or otherwise have chosen a play along with a specific character to analyze within that play. That said, many exercises can be repeated as needed in order to explore multiple characters which may be beneficial for those who are analyzing a text from the perspective of a director or designer. We've also suggested modifications to certain exercises to allow them to serve a broader analysis of the play.

Our Approach

Our tools are not entirely new. Throughout the book we will reference Konstantin Stanislavski's ideas as laid out in *An Actor's Work* translated by Jean Benedetti. Any page reference to Stanislavski is a reference to that text which is a wonderful companion text to this book. Our purpose is not to simply update Stanislavski's ideas. Instead, we want to acknowledge that the previous script analysis texts that use Stanislavski's concepts could do more to make space for actors who are not straight, white, cisgender, able-bodied, middle to upper class, and mostly males. We envision character analysis that is more attentive to and inclusive of experiences that are not traditionally represented in acting texts of this kind.

In order to assist in this process, we'll draw from a range of theoretical resources in each chapter. Each theory is matched in a chapter to a specific component of character development. This does not mean we encourage you to think about these theoretical frameworks only in connection with their particular chapter. Rather, we hope that they accumulate over chapters, complicating your analysis of characters all the while.

You'll probably quickly note that we separate different aspects of identity in each chapter in order to focus on them specifically, too. In reality, of course, this isn't possible. The components of one's identity intermingle and intertwine with one another. In certain circumstances, one aspect may be felt especially keenly, or two aspects may create an undeniable tension in a given moment, but they all reside together in you just as they will in a character. Be attentive, therefore, to the way aspects of identity intersect.

It's also worth noting that, while this text seeks to structure a more inclusive character analysis geared for a college-aged actor, it doesn't directly offer inclusive strategies for teaching or participating in a college classroom. Nevertheless, we offer some suggestions that are in keeping with the overall content of this book. Consider the following:

- We all approach one another with preconceived notions, expectations, and stereotypes about who the other person is. This is particularly true with visible markers of identity. We can often unwittingly foist these expectations on one another. Even seemingly positive stereotypes can be damaging. Don't assume you're above this, otherwise you'll have a hard time keeping these notions in check.
- You can't expect a person who identifies with a particular group to answer for all persons in that group. Even if a student willingly offers insights into their experience, it's not fair to burden them with guiding you through every question that occurs to you or to presume they have some kind of all-encompassing reference book guiding them.
- You'll get things wrong, or someone else will get something wrong. When it is you who is in the wrong, have the humility to admit it, apologize, and learn. When others harm, take the time to address the harm by discussing the cause and the impact. Resolve to do better.
- Give people space to be who they are. Be grateful when they want to share who they are with you. Listen openly. If we are to amplify more voices, that might well mean talking less ourselves.
- Theoretical conversations will continue to shift, and new language will evolve. There are theoretical frames not included in this text. The suggested reading lists are limited. This book is a starting point, not an ending point. Continue to learn and engage with the conversations and changes in language and theory.

While this text focuses on inclusive theatre and acting techniques rather than strategies for creating an inclusive classroom, it is our belief that opening the dialogue and bringing diverse viewpoints into the conversation through critical theory will be an act of inclusion.

Further Reading

Dolan, Jill. "Geographies of Learning: Theatre Studies, Performance, and the 'Performative.' *Theatre Journal*, vol. 45, no.4, 1993, pp, 417–441.

Stanislavski, Konstantin and Jean Benedetti. *An Actor's Work: A Student's Diary*. New York: Routledge, 2008.

Chapter 1

Reading the Language of the Play

This chapter introduces the reader to foundational script reading tactics. Additionally, this chapter reminds readers to check in on their own expectations and assumptions about the script. Finally, the first step in analysis is to engage the playwright's language for basic understanding as well as historical or cultural context, and social awareness.

Words are our entry point into analyzing the play. In each chapter, we will build our understanding of the play and its characters by exploring different concepts which illuminate one facet or another about the play. These concepts always use the raw material of the play's text, its words. For example, in Chapter 3, we will learn given circumstances (or the facts of the play) from the text, which can then point us to research. Additionally, we can deduce the characters' desires and subsequent actions based on the words they speak, as we will explore in Chapter 5. As both of these examples suggest, language is our entry point to a character's inner life; their ideas, values, beliefs, and feelings are suggested if not outright stated through their words. Because so much rests on our interpretation of what is spoken by characters, it's important to begin with a special focus on words. Subsequent chapters will deepen the work begun here.

This chapter will challenge you to recognize and investigate the assumptions and biases you bring to play reading and will provide new ways to think about analyzing and understanding plays. Sure, you've read a hundred plays (or a thousand if you are faculty), but who taught you to read a play and what assumptions or biases were embedded in those teachings? This chapter creates space to investigate the habits you have developed or new ways to think about reading plays.

The Title

Before you even open the script (or swipe the screen), take some time to think about the title. The title isn't something to skip over or to ignore. It is our first introduction to the world of the play, the author's first word(s) to the reader/viewer, and the first place for us to check in on assumptions. What are you bringing to the table before you even crack open the spine? The first rule—there are no rules and there are no wrong answers. What you are doing is checking in with your gut, your connections (social or cultural), and your preconceived knowledge of the script.

Exercise 1.1: A Title is Intentional

Before you start reading any script, make sure you take five minutes to reflect and freewrite on the title. Here are a few questions to get you started.

- What image or actions does the title evoke?
- Are there hints to a theme or major idea?
- Does the title create an emotional or physical response for you?
- Have you heard of the title before?
- What assumptions or associations with the title do you bring to this reading?

As an example, here are some questions to explore using *A Raisin in the Sun* by Lorraine Hansberry. What does the title sound like or look like? Do you like raisins? Has it been gloomy and dark out for the last 10 days and you are longing for sunshine? Have you read "Harlem" by Langston Hughes and that phrase recalls memories of a high school classroom?

All of these things may seem small and arbitrary, but taking even a few minutes to jot down a few connections or associations with the title connects you to your own biases or expectations as you open the script.

The Character List

Exploring the character list can be a treasure trove of information. Take the time to read the character list and think about the hints and keys the playwright is offering to the reader. Who is this script about? What relationships can you make out? What other facts or assumptions can you discern from the list?

Exercise 1.2: What's in a Name?

As we did with the title, take five minutes to reflect and freewrite on the character list. Here are a few questions to get you started.

- Are the names familiar to you? Why or why not?
- Is there any indication of relationships?
- Are there any historical markers or indications?
- Are there names that seem connected and/or names that indicate a "difference"?
- Are there any characters that are diminished or elevated in any way? What does that indicate about them in the play?
- Do you know anyone with any of these names? If so, how do you feel about that name?
- What other cultural, social, or personal responses do you have to the list of characters?

Sticking with Hansberry's *A Raisin in the Sun* as an example, what can we gather from the list of characters?

> Ruth Younger
> Travis Younger
> Walter Lee Younger (Brother)
> Beneatha Younger
> Lena Younger (Mama)
> Joseph Asagai
> George Murchison
> Bobo
> Karl Lindner
> Two Moving Men

At first glance, there are several "observations" we can make about the characters in the play. First, several individuals have the same surname and two of those are referenced as being related, which might mean we can assume the others are related as well. Next, Bobo doesn't have a last name, which may indicate something about his social standing. We may also have a response to a character with a name like Bobo. The indication that there are "unnamed" characters who are identified solely as "moving men" may give us an indication of potential action in the play.

Taking the time to familiarize yourself with potential relationships and/or responses or reactions to character names, identities, or relationships is an important way to make sure you are allowing the characters to freely introduce themselves to you.

Stage Directions

Many of us have a bad habit of jumping right into the text of a script and bypassing the vital italics of stage directions or setting that include important nuggets of information for us to take into the opening lines of dialogue. *A Raisin in the Sun* begins with:

> Time: The early 1950s
> Place: Chicago's Southside

Even before we go into the specifics of what the interior of the Younger's house looks like, Hansberry gives us information to think about and reflect on. What do we know about the 1950s? What are our assumptions about the time period, the look, and the experiences? What do we know about Chicago's Southside either contemporarily or from the 1950s? Think about how this knowledge or lack of knowledge can impact how you begin to read the play.

If you are only reading the play once, take the time now to go and look up the background information that you need to understand the context of the play. For this play, what are the demographics of Chicago's Southside? What do you need to know about the 1950s and its relationship to the area? If you know you are going to read the play more than once, sometimes it is good to read the play without doing this research and jump directly to the next step outlined below.

Elements of Plot

Typically, plots are structured linearly (meaning the action moves forward and sequentially in time) and causally (meaning one action causes another action). In these structures, there are several elements that contribute to the structure, and thus, the meaning of the play. The primary elements include exposition, inciting incident, rising action, and climax.

Exposition is the background information the playwright offers the readers about the characters, their lives, their dwelling, and their world. Exposition helps us understand the world of the play. Look for this information in the opening stage directions or in the first few scenes. This is typically not dramatized action, but instead clues that help us understand relationships, histories, and contexts.

The inciting incident is the moment that sets the play's conflict into motion. You can check to see if you have identified the inciting incident by removing the moment from the script. Removing the inciting incident removes the conflict, which is central to any story, and results in little meaningful action left in the script.

Rising actions are the moments that continue to build up tension and emotional intensity in the world of the play. These incremental actions are smaller obstacles or discoveries that raise the stakes for the characters.

As the rising actions build, they lead to the climax of the play, which is the emotional high point, when the conflict is decided or resolved.

Understanding how the elements of plot work together to create the structure of the play is important; this is the map or framework the playwright provides to understand the world of the play. Your understanding and identification of these moments will impact how you interpret the meaning of the play.

Reading the Play

We offer a few tips to help you engage fully with the script as you sit down to read. Before we start, here are some general notes to consider about space and time.

- Prepare a comfortable space to read. Preferably sit up with access to a writing space.
- Eliminate or minimize distractions. This means noise-cancelling headphones, no television or music playing in the background, etc.
- Allow yourself enough time to read the play in a single sitting.

Remember that you aren't reading for pleasure or entertainment. It is a different kind of reading. You are a detective or researcher exploring the text for clues, contexts, and history.

Next, try to read, imagine, and enter the world that has been offered to you by the playwright. Engage, ask questions, feel and respond to the work in your hands. Check in with yourself if you are resistant to a character or relationship or a way a character speaks. This resistance is a good moment to check in on your expectations or biases. Is there a personal connection or discomfort clouding your experience of the play? This is often unavoidable, but we must be aware of how our own experiences or expectations are framing our understanding and interpretation of the script.

Finally, as you read, make sure you are either taking the time to look up words or situations you don't know or understand or write down questions to research following the first read. This seems obvious, but don't just ignore words you are unfamiliar with, places you couldn't identify on a map, or phrases that feel foreign to you. Take the time to make notes (along with page number) or to do the research as you read.

Exercise 1.3: The No-Shame, Personal Glossary

No one's understanding of their own language or history is complete. Our vocabulary and our knowledge of culturally specific references, for example, all depends on our life experiences. There is no shame in not knowing a word, historical situation, cultural moment, etc. Don't be embarrassed to seek out the information that will deepen your understanding of a character's world. Those words and experiences are a part of them, and you are working to know them in a very deep and intimate way.

This exercise will help you generate a glossary of any words or experiences you feel fit from one of the categories below. As with many exercises in this text, you can use this activity to focus on one character, or all characters from the text depending on your goals. Be ready to use several sheets of paper, at least a new one for every category. Leave plenty of space in between words or questions, especially if you are going to list all words first and define later. Finally, note page numbers so that you can quickly refer back to these words.

Category One: New to me. Words or experiences I don't know specific definitions for or understandings of.

Here, list and define every word or experience your character speaks or hears for which you don't have a specific definition or that you simply don't know but need to learn. If you analyze the script more broadly, as a director or a designer might, you should be sure to define all the words, references, or experiences with which you are unfamiliar.

Category Two: Familiar but uncertain. Words or experiences I recognize but am not certain I know.

Here, list and define words or experiences that you may recognize or even be familiar with but aren't fully confident about their definition or history. Remember, if you focus on one character, you'll need a specific understanding of the words or experiences they are using or referencing.

Code words. Words or experiences that the character uses or hears that convey an unexpected meaning.

These are words or experiences that mask a secondary or veiled meaning. A code word is meant to convey one thing to someone who is "in the know" and something different to anyone else who overhears it. This hidden meaning is disguised by a second definition, so list and define both. For example, the phrase "Operation Licorice" acts as a code word with little to no meaning for anyone who doesn't know the story the phrase references. For two characters, however, it reminds them of a story that involved an ambitious, fun excursion for licorice ice cream that turned into a chaotic fiasco. When these two characters whisper "operation licorice" to one another a shared understanding passes between them that no other character is privy to.

Personal Associations. Words or experiences that mean more to the character than their definition expresses.

Here, list and define words or experiences that seem to have special significance and meaning to a given character.

Let the definition or history be that character's personal association with that word. Unlike code words or experiences, that definition or history may be felt or experienced by the character, but the language isn't coded as in the previous section. If you explore multiple characters, be sure to list the character name beside the personal association.

You may find other categories for your glossary. If so, add pages in the same manner. This glossary may grow as you explore your character, particularly as you realize that character has certain personal associations with words. There is no correct amount of words for this glossary, so don't concern yourself with whether you have more or fewer words than others.

When you've finished reading the play, take a few minutes to write down your initial responses. Some questions to get you started include:

- Was this play what you were expecting? If not, what were you expecting and why?
- Is there a character that you connect with particularly? If so, how does that impact your interpretation? Likewise, is there a character you are strongly resistant to and how does that impact your interpretation?
- What questions do you still have about the characters or the action of the play?
- If you were to imagine a scene after the end of the play, what do you think happens?
- What is a two-sentence description of the play?

Your Next Read-throughs: Unpacking the Language

You will re-read the play several times over the course of your work with it. These subsequent readings will allow you to focus on the words the playwright uses to craft the world of the play. Understanding the words, in all their layers of meaning, is how we begin to understand the world of the play and the characters.

Characters use words to give shape to their thoughts, express their emotions, and to influence others. They speak to make desires known with the hope that doing so will help get them what they want, or to persuade someone to act in a way that helps rather than hinders them. If nothing else, they make their thoughts and feelings known out of a desire *to be known* by someone else, which is fundamental to the human experience. Speaking helps characters to achieve some goal. Itis rarely a simple act carried out just for the sake of filling a silence.

If speaking is most often an action directed at some goal, then we must determine what action the character intends and to what end. For that to happen, we need a specific understanding of the word's meaning as well as an understanding of what the character understands that word to mean (which is not necessarily the same thing). We should assume that the character has chosen a word specifically, even though this may not always be the case, and so intends to convey a specific meaning through it. So, first, you'll need to know the meanings of any words your character speaks. This may seem obvious, but I want to stress this point here because we sometimes allow ourselves to get by with an approximate understanding of a word. Sometimes, we even operate with an entirely inaccurate definition of a word. Learning the precise definition of a word often comes to an actor as a revelation, deepening their understanding of a character's intentions or thoughts. So, any word your character speaks (or hears for that matter) that you are not entirely certain the meaning of, you should define.

Of course, words aren't static and unchanging things. Rather, their meanings shift and change depending on certain factors. Over time and in different contexts words can accumulate and shed meanings. You need only to look at a seemingly simple word like "cool" to see the way a word's meaning changes dramatically depending on who says it, in what way they say it, and when and where they say it. When you analyze the words a character uses, consider whether there are factors at play that transform the word's meaning.

Characters may have personal associations with certain words, too. Their feelings and opinions may be attached to specific words in a way that is unique to them. These associations don't exactly change the meaning of a word so much as complicate it. Characters use such words to express more than just that word's literal meaning. They express some subtle undercurrent of their thoughts at the same time. These could be code words with which a character expresses some shared meaning to another like when someone explains the relationship of two people by saying, "Oh them, they're good *friends*" using that special emphasis on "friends" to indicate that there's a lot more going on between those two than simple friendship.

Or consider, for example, two characters who have dramatically different experiences with love; experiences that give them very different opinions on it. Let's say the first has been lucky in love. They are optimistic about it; they view it as a connective force benevolently pulling people together. The second disagrees. They find the whole notion of love silly, seeing instead the delusions of immature fools tricking themselves about the meaning of their emotions. When the first says "love," they mean something else, and so probably speak it with an entirely different attitude than the second.

All of this is to say that in order to understand a character, you must understand their words because those words give you some of the deepest insight you'll find about who they are. Those words, once defined, lend clarity to a character's thoughts and intentions. Once they are particularly defined for that character, they add more detail to their opinions and emotional expressions. They are a primary means for building a character's *particular point of view*.

Taking the time to dig into the playwright's choice of words (both characters' lines and the stage directions) is our first step into the more detailed work of character analysis.

All the theatrical elements that help to realize a full performance take their cue from the spoken text and the stage directions. In the upcoming sections, we'll introduce ways that you can return to the text with one special focus or another.

Choosing Your Words

The particular words a character uses when they speak are probably not accidental, so assume there is a reason the character chooses a given word. Sometimes, word choice is a matter of signaling affiliation or identity. Maybe the character identifies with a particular group, and so, adopts the jargon, slang, and verbal norms of that group. Word choice may also signal ideology, values, or priorities. Perhaps the character values simplicity and given the choice will use a common word before using an esoteric one. Or, maybe they convey a love for nature by employing nature metaphors at every turn.

The words a character uses reveal something about their particular point of view. Take time to consider what the character signals about their background, social groups, ideals, and preferences when they use particular words. If patterns start to emerge, then trust that those patterns are part of who the character is.

Exercise 1.4: Revealing Words

Use this exercise for one character at a time. Repeat as needed if you analyze several characters.

Look over the words that your character uses. Are their related words or short phrases that you could categorize under some simple heading? For example, "Machine Jargon," "Words Borrowed from Spanish," or "Bookish Words." If you see a pattern of words or phrases that could fit a category that seems important to understand the character, collect those words together by writing them out on the top half of a blank page.

On the bottom half of that page, write a bit about what you think this pattern suggests. Does it suggest something about the character's daily experience in a repair shop? Is it an intentional signaling of the character's Latinx identity? Are they an unconscious expression of the character's education? See what conclusions you can draw about the character through their word choice. Then, consider what implications that has for playing or understanding the character.

Structure

The thoughts and emotions of a character are often revealed as much through the way their lines are constructed as they are through the specific meaning of each individual word. Their emotions, carried on the voice and in between the words, can be conveyed in a series of pauses indicated by ellipses or the rushing flow of a run-on sentence. The structure of lines can convey the thoughts of a character or the outpouring of their emotional state, so it is useful to consider the patterns of words (and silences) that the lines suggest when taken all together. In this section, we'll look at some factors that will help illuminate these patterns.

- *Punctuation*
  - Consider what the punctuation suggests about the way a line could be expressed. Does the sentence end in the emotive rush of an exclamation point? Does the character vocally lift what would normally be a declarative by adding a question mark to the end?

  How does internal punctuation shape the line's flow? Consider, for example, the difference between:
  "Listen, I have something I need to tell you."
  ...and
  "Listen. I... have something... I need to tell you."

Internal commas, dashes, and ellipses might weave a line of verbal tangents together, suggest a rapid accumulation of thoughts being crammed into a small space, or let clause after clause meander around while the character struggles to nail down just what it is they are trying to express. Treat punctuation as cues signaling the directions within the line.

- *Sequence*
  - The order of the thoughts in your character's lines can yield a great deal of information about a character's state of mind. Some characters build one thought on top of another, laying out a logical sequence in the hopes of leading someone else down a specific path. Others dart about just trying to gather together thoughts that spiral out in different directions, hopping back and forth between ideas. Perhaps, they set up one possibility only to knock it down a moment later, disregarding one idea after another in the search for some conclusion.

Take for example this sequence of thoughts:

I had a really bad day.
   I woke up with a head cold.
   I stubbed my toe getting out of bed.
   By the time I got my clothes on I realized I missed a meeting.
   The meeting was with my boss about a promotion at work.
   So, I'm definitely not getting promoted!

Often characters create an emotional build by laying out a foundational idea ("I had a really bad day."), then amplifying with a succession of related ideas that build to a pinnacle thought ("So, I'm definitely not getting promoted!"). This amplification works something like a set of stairs or a ladder. Whatever the emotional tenor, each step increases the intensity and takes the character a little bit closer to the culmination of that emotion.

- *Comparisons and Contrasts*
  - Making comparisons and contrasts is a common tactic when trying to explain something unfamiliar by likening it to something more familiar. The acts of comparison and contrast have different qualities to them which the character can reinforce vocally. Paying attention to whether a character is setting two ideas in opposition or highlighting their similarity is helpful for determining both what a character is saying and how they may say it. A character may be crafting a metaphor because they are talking about a concept that is abstract (excitement, anger, sorrow), and so, they express their thoughts or feelings by likening the abstract concept to something more tangible and concrete (a rush of water, a rage of fire, an echo in an empty room). They can reinforce that similarity vocally by making the concepts literally *sound* similar when they speak them. Conversely, a character may be setting up a tension between two oppositional concepts (love and hate, more and less, kind and cruel) which they can reinforce vocally as well.

Here are two examples:

Comparison
"I'm so excited to go dancing tonight, I feel like I've been walking around with springs in my heels all day!"
Here the character can create a vocal resonance in their tone (perhaps a higher than usual pitch in their voice) as they say "excited" and "springs in my heels"
Contrast
Alternatively, the same character might see the unenthusiastic responses of their friends and say, "I can't

believe everyone can stay so calm when I feel like bouncing!"

Here the character can create a tonal contrast with the same pitch for "bouncing" they used before, but a lower tone and slower delivery as they say "so calm"

- *Silence*
  - It may sound cliché, but it is nevertheless true that silence often speaks volumes. Think about what provokes a pause. What lingers in the air after a sentence that trails off? What words or expressions of emotion pass through a shared glance? These silences can be just as important as what a character manages to put into words. It's worth considering why a character doesn't speak in certain key moments. Is there something that they long to say but fear to put into words? Maybe there is an understanding between some characters and their silence is comfortable. Maybe it's necessary. Just because they don't give it voice, there may be quite a bit of monolog running through a character's mind.

A simple example of a loaded silence between characters might be something like:

"Well, you could try it, but last time… *(silence)* Well you remember…"

Here the silence carries an implicit warning against some action based on shared memory.

Exercise 1.5: Visualizing the Structure

Use this exercise for one character at a time and for particular sections of the text. Repeat as needed if you analyze several characters.

If possible, find a large amount of text that your character speaks with little or no interruption from others. You could also look at a sampling of shorter lines or simply find a monolog from another play for this exercise. Write the text out sentence-by-sentence with some space in between lines. Let sentence fragments stand as a line on their own.

Beneath each line, draw a visual representation of that text's flow. The visual representation should be done in a way that makes sense to you and captures something of the tone structure of the line. Try to capture its twists and turns, its builds and drops, if applicable. Try to capture its tempo and rhythm—slow and regular? Sporadic and rapid? Sudden change mid-line?

You might use colors or a system of symbols. Musicians may want to use musical notation (crescendos, decrescendos, forte, and piano). The main thing is for you to try and see how a line flows and how that flow relates to the entirety of what the character says. What does this visualization reveal? How does it shape your understanding of what is going on for the character in that moment?

This exercise can be repeated as necessary. It doesn't even require a large chunk of text. Sometimes, looking at the shape of a single line helps you learn more about what the character is trying to express, how they manage it, and what that all says about who they are. This is a great activity to do with a line or passage that is giving you trouble. Sometimes the move from words to image opens up new meanings and interpretations.

Subtext

Even as they speak them, the words themselves are only a part of what a character conveys in the act of speaking. Beneath the text is a roiling current of *subtext*. Subtext, or *the meaning that is expressed beneath the lines*, gives the text a particular shape and feel. It may be a matter of conveying true feelings from behind a facade of otherwise harmless words, as in a character who says "funny that we keep running into each other" while implying with their tone that they are not at all pleased. Or, a character might suggest that what they are saying is an understatement, as in a character who gently tests the water with "I really enjoy hanging out with you" while a barely contained *Oh god, I think I'm in love with you* bubbles underneath.

It may be that fear restricts their ability to say what they really feel; it may be that social norms forbid a character from directly expressing their thoughts. Perhaps, they are simply incapable of expressing everything that is going on inside. Whatever the reason, characters very often leave a great deal unsaid within their lines. Nevertheless, the subtext changes the tone, stresses a particular word, or otherwise colors the line so that the subterranean thoughts and feelings are heard. It is our job to discover and unpack the subtext.

Exercise 1.6: Subtext Translations

In groups of four, decide one of you will be Actor A and another Actor B. The remaining two will provide subtext for either A or B. You can rotate these roles as often as you need, but at the very least, be sure you've tried speaking Text and Subtext. Use the lines as text.

First, Actor A will speak a line to Actor B. Next, Subtext A "translates" that line by suggesting the subtext. Actor A now repeats that line allowing the subtext that their partner has suggested to shape the delivery. Then, Actor B tries a line and the pattern repeats.

At first, don't worry about making a scene, so Actor B doesn't need to respond to A's line. Instead, you're just experimenting with the way subtext shapes text. You might even choose the same line over and over with new suggestions of subtext each time. There is a tendency in this game for the subtext to suggest that the line is a sarcastic one and the character essentially means the exact opposite of what they say. This is not a "wrong" or "bad" choice, but remember that it is not the only choice. It may not even be the most interesting one.

To get you started, try this first line and a few of the suggested subtexts beneath it. After that, move on to the rest of the text experimenting with ideas of your own.

Text:
Hello. How have you been?
Subtext Options:

- *Oh, I've missed you so much!*
- *Please don't mention our last awkward conversation.*
- *Do I know you?*
- *You look amazing.*
- *I'm really not in the mood to chit chat.*
- *I just heard a very juicy rumor about you.*

Here are some more lines you might try adding subtext to:

- I'm so glad you made it.
- There you are.
- I haven't seen you in a while.
- I've been thinking a lot about you.
- You always have something interesting to say.
- What have you been doing lately?
- Where did you get that _____? (bird, outfit, joke, dance move, sandwich, etc.)
- I'm glad we had this time together.
- I hope I get to see you again soon.

After some practice with the pattern, you could try improvising a short scene in this way. Agree on a simple scenario, relationship, and location. Pick a line to begin with and simply see where it goes. Remember to listen and simply accept suggestions from each other, discovering how a change in subtext impacts the meaning of the text.

Word into Action

When characters speak, they perform an action through their words; an action which is usually a further attempt to fulfill their needs. Rarely do characters speak something neutrally. When analyzing a character's lines, ask why they bother speaking at all. What do they hope to get from speaking? What is the action being performed? What are they doing with their words?

Very often, when actors are asked what they are *doing* with a line, they respond, "I'm telling her this," or "I'm asking him that." While true enough, "telling," "saying," "asking," and other general words that describe the act of speaking lack the specificity and detail actors should aim for when they consider actions. So, when you are wondering why a character speaks at all, remember what they are trying to get and what they are going to do to get it. Is simply asking enough? Do they need to demand instead? Beg? Or perhaps the character is performing a bit themselves, asking something they know the answer to in order to make someone else squirm.

Often, a character expresses themselves so they can share something that is happening internally that they do not want to keep inside. It is important to remember that in these moments, the action *to be*, as in to be happy or to be hurt, is still too passive for playing the role, and simply *telling* another character how they feel is too general. The emotion is felt and even generated or made more powerful as a result of a specific action. That is, a character opens up, or vents, or begs for sympathy, or celebrates. As a result of those actions, their emotions become more vibrant and possibly even shared. The emotional expression may even move the character toward fulfilling a desire, as in "I want to feel close to this other character, so I will let my joy burst out of me and hope that it infects them with laughter." The emotion, then, is a byproduct of expressive actions and circumstances, not the action itself.

If a character is *telling* another character something that happened or how they feel about events, consider why they want to tell their story at all. What do they want from the listener? Then, let that turn the general act of *telling* into something more specific. Perhaps, they want to impress their audience and will paint a vivid picture with their words. Maybe they have to convince someone by making an argument and will carefully take them from point to point, always checking to see if the listener is following. They could be trying to excite, terrify, encourage, warn, or vent. When you know what it is your character wants from a specific moment, asking how specifically they will use their words to get it will help you turn words into action.

Maintaining Curiosity

Getting to know a script and a character in the kind of depth that this analysis requires will mean reading and re-reading the play several times. This can be a daunting prospect in a way because it requires a great deal of mental energy if those repeated readings are going to be productive. Your reading shouldn't be a matter of simply dragging your eyes across the same words over and over as you memorize them. Rather, it requires you to maintain curiosity about a play that you've already read several times. Assume that the play can still surprise you. Read as if there is a hidden detail that you missed last time. A great play can continue to reveal something new about itself even after several readings. Read like you're reading a great play. Enjoy the journey.

Further Reading

Moseley, Nick. "Subtext." *Acting and Reacting: Tools for the Modern Actor.* London: Nick Hern Books, 2006.

Wainscott, Ronald and Kathy Fletcher. "Understanding the Play: A Theatrical Blueprint." *Theatre: Collaborative Acts*, 4th edition. New Jersey: Pearson, 2012.

Quick Definitions

Climax: Emotional highpoint of the play; the point at which the central character or characters are closest to achieving their goals, but are still at risk for losing it all.

Exposition: Background information that helps you understand the world of the play.

Inciting incident: The moment that sets the conflict in motion.

Rising action: Small units of action that raise the levels of intensity leading to the climax.

Subtext: The meaning that is expressed beneath a character's lines.

Chapter 2

Standpoint Theory and If

This chapter explores Stanislavksi's If as an initiator of empathy and how we understand the world and lives of characters. Understanding our own perceptions of the world through our social, cultural, and identity groups is important to self-understanding. As we understand our own social location, it helps us to understand how we see the world. Using standpoint theory as a frame, this chapter looks to widen the scope of possibilities for our world and the worlds of our characters.

Sympathy and Empathy

While this chapter is centered around the imaginative act of asking If, we first need to establish a shared understanding of empathy.

To begin, a short story to help explore sympathy and empathy:

At a park near home, I seek out a quiet spot off a bend in the path. This spot is sheltered by a tree and a bit overgrown all around, so it's easy to disappear from view. There, I decide to enjoy some privacy and read, or at least pretend to. I'm not out there long before I hear, what is unmistakably, crying nearby. I can't see the crier, and they likely don't know I am there. I may not know who they are, but I feel pity welling inside for them when I hear them openly weeping.

Wondering whether I should help or at least make my presence known, I decide to come slowly around the trunk of the tree. On the other side, I see the erratic rise and fall of shoulders and hands partially covering a face. I slowly recognize my friend. Feeling a closeness to them, I suddenly feel that pity deepening into something more. I am moved by their display of sadness and can't help but feel a sadness of my own at the sight.

Fortunately, my friend is not embarrassed by their public display of emotion and expresses that running into me is a relief. I try to console my friend, but quickly find it best to listen. Even as I listen to the details pouring out, I can't help but imagine myself in similar circumstances, imagining myself going through the same thing. Soon, we are both crying. This feeling is different than when I initially recognized my friend in their sorrow because it comes from a deeper understanding of my friend's circumstances. In a strange way, the sadness I feel now is both my own and not my own.

We gather up our belongings and venture off in search of food. We go to a place that makes really great tacos and things get better quickly.

It's not uncommon to hear *sympathy* and *empathy* used interchangeably. Both words describe an emotional encounter in which one person's emotions affect another person's emotions. In sympathy and empathy this happens to such a degree that the second person's emotional state is transformed by the first person's emotional state, as happens in the story above. Sympathy and empathy even have a way of feeding into one another, so it makes sense that the distinctions between the two get lost. For theatre, and for acting in particular, marking the difference between the two clarifies something vital about what it is to inhabit a role.

An older word, sympathy has accrued multiple meanings over the years, but generally suggests harmony that is usually brought about by a sense of similarity or closeness. As an emotional response, if I feel sympathy, I am affected by the emotions and situations of another and may feel similarly as a result. Sympathy may involve pity, but is usually a stronger emotional experience overall.

Importantly, in feeling sympathy for someone else, I don't necessarily feel those emotions with the same intensity as they do. I may not feel them at all. Though I may be drawn into sadness by my friend's sorrow, I may also retain a compassionate distance. Similarly, I may feel agitated by another's righteous anger or bubbly at another's leaping joy, but there remains a distance. Sympathy is more like a dance in which one partner moves in a complementary way to another, but the bodies remain separate.

Sympathy is a vital human response for anyone who wants to develop intimacy with others. It can bond people, lead to advocacy, or simply provide some much-needed listening and support. However, an actor typically needs more than sympathy to inhabit a role. An actor must not only harmonize with the character but also blend so fully with their character so as to be one voice with them. They need *empathy*.

Feeling empathy suggests adopting someone else's attitude, a process of inserting yourself into another's perspective so fully that you can both understand them and feel as they do. Through empathy, I feel as another does. This is not only because of our closeness but also because I have imaginatively taken on their circumstances *as if they were my own*. I have used my imagination to adopt their point of view, allowing me to feel in some way what they feel. For an actor, the aim is to allow this empathetic process to provide a channel into the lived experience of a character, helping the actor to feel and more easily behave as that character would. This chapter, along with Chapter 3, will establish practices to enable empathy.

As we begin imagining the ways we can understand empathy and sympathy for our characters, it is important to remember that our own social groups can offer boundaries that promote safety and comfort, but can also form bias and suspicion if left unchecked.

Understanding standpoint theory is helpful in unpacking sympathy and empathy in our characters as well as examining our own connections to social groups. Standpoint theory joined theoretical conversations in the 1970s and 1980s and has gone through several re-investigations and re-interpretations. The basic premise of standpoint theory investigates the relationship between "production of knowledge and practices of power" (Harding 1). The argument is that those who make knowledge (research institutions, government groups, policy makers, etc.) hold the most social, cultural, and capital power. Standpoint theory is most helpful for character analysis in remembering groups of people experience the world in different ways based on their social location, or their position in social or cultural groups. Keeping the connection between "groups" and "power" offered by standpoint theory, what gender did you imagine the characters in the example above? Why? What words/images/indications in the example above led you to that determination? What about your own social groups may have contributed to your conclusion?

Not sure about your standpoint? Here is an exercise to help you.

Exercise 2.1: I Am, I Am Not

Take out a piece of paper and write "I Am…" at the top of the left-hand side of the page. Spend 3–5 minutes filling in your "I am" statements with identity and group markers. Examples could be:

I am left-handed.
I am a woman.
I am queer.
I am Catholic.
I am fat.
I am white.

Complete the "I am" statements without judgement or embarrassment. These are the identities and groups that you hold and/or belong to.

After you have filled your page, draw a line down the middle and mark "I Am Not..." on the top of the right-hand side of the page. Write the corresponding "I am not" statement to each of your "I am" statements. Again, don't think or overanalyze, just write the first corresponding statement that comes to mind. For example:

I am left-handed.	I am not right-handed.
I am a woman.	I am not a man.
I am queer.	I am not straight.
I am Catholic.	I am not an atheist.
I am fat.	I am not skinny.
I am white.	I am not BIPOC.
I am a student.	I am not a professor.

You might have had different connections for these "I am/I am not" statement examples. That is perfectly fine. How we create the opposition statement tells us what groups or identities we think are at odds or different from ourselves. This is influenced by our history, by our background, and by our socialization. The person sitting next to you could write different "I Am Not" responses to every one of your "I Am" statements.

After you have finished your "I Am Not" statements, go through each pairing and identify which statement holds the position of power.

I am left-handed.	**I am not right-handed.**
I am a woman.	**I am not a man.**
I am queer.	**I am not straight.**
I am Catholic.	I am not an atheist.
I am fat.	**I am not skinny**.
I am white.	I am not BIPOC.
I am a student.	**I am not a professor.**

Take note of whether your identity contains more privilege or subordination to a dominant group or identity.

Understanding the social groups and/or identities that you belong to and which groups or identities hold power is important. Your social location and standpoint inform how you see the world. Understanding that we may be resistant to certain identities or ideas because they threaten our position of power is important to understanding the world and the worlds of our characters. If we feel threatened or challenged by an idea or identity that our characters hold, we must be aware of how our own biases or status color our understanding of the world of the play.

This exercise can be completed for our characters as well.

As our "I Am" and "I Am Not" lists indicate, our understanding of the world is largely based on this somewhat simplistic, but important, list of statements. It is critical to understand and remember that we assess the world with a particular viewpoint and likewise, the world responds to us in a particular way, depending on the "group[s]" society places us in. Patricia Hill Collins explains standpoint as referring "to groups having shared histories based on their shared location in relations of power" (248). The groups that we share histories and experiences with are important—as a woman you have some understanding of what other women experience. And yet, standpoint also reminds us that "different bodies are subjected to different material conditions and forces that can give rise to different experiences and thus different evidence and beliefs" (Intemann 785). This means that while you, as a woman, might have similar experiences or common understanding with other women. However if you are a wealthy, white, physically fit woman, your experiences will differ from a woman who is also white and physically fit, but lives in poverty.

Before moving on, it is important to note that not everyone feels empathy for others easily, or at all. Our minds and bodies are diverse, and some will find that they have barriers to empathy for reasons spanning from neurologically rooted difficulty to habitual inattention to others. Theatre artists are not all made from the same neurological mold and may find that they need to work at empathy. Some may need to find another way into character entirely.

Studies suggest that empathy or empathetic behaviors can be taught (see Teding van Berkhout and Malouff), which suggests that your starting point is not necessarily your ending point in feeling empathy. So, this exercise may help establish a foundation, regardless of your current empathetic capacities. Building on the previous exercise, the next exercise will help you build a bridge between self and character, examining your social location first in order to better find similarities between you and someone else.

Exercise 2.2: Beginning an Emotional Inventory

Empathy requires a perspective shift in which you imaginatively take on the circumstances of another as if they were your own. You may find it easier to understand what is provoking strong emotions in someone else if you already have a firm understanding of what provokes strong emotions in you. Answering the questions below will help you get started.

The questions here are not intended to help you recreate memories, although some will certainly have memories attached to them. Rather, they are meant to help you generate hypotheticals, things that could provoke strong feelings if they were to happen. This list will not comprehensively map your emotional territory, but it should get you acquainted with some major landmarks. This exercise can be used to explore the emotional inventory of your character as well. Try providing a few answers to each section even if you don't answer every question fully right away.

What and who are important to you? Who do you care about deeply and why? What ideas do you value? What ideas do you oppose? Are there people in your life that you emulate? People who you try to avoid behaving like? Are there people you trust? Are there people you love?

Who are the people you would be excited to see? What are activities that would exhilarate you if you were going to do them later? What ideas excite you? Places? Clothes? Foods? What makes you laugh?

What or who would you be sad to lose if they were gone? Who could hurt you if they were ashamed of you or no longer wanted to see you? What ideas bring you low? Would someone's death or absence be particularly painful to you?

What are your fears? What would terrify you if it were to happen? What worries you? What are you concerned about possibly happening in your life?

What is awe inspiring to you? What would inspire wonder if you were to experience it? What stops you in your tracks? What starts your imagination working?

At any point, take something from the list you've generated here and expand on it. Ask yourself why any item is emotionally charged for you or get specific about the circumstances of one of these hypotheticals. The more you do this, the more concrete knowledge you have about your emotional life.

Again, this list does not address all that you are capable of feeling or experiencing, but it should get you started on a very important task—knowing your emotional territory. If you know yourself, you might better be able to know a character by drawing parallels between the things that provoke emotions in you and what provokes emotion in them. While your experiences are still likely to be quite different, you can find commonalities through which you can build a bridge from your perspective and theirs.

Empathy for Characters

Empathy is equally possible with another living and breathing person as it is with a fictitious character living only on the page. What is important is not so much whether the circumstances are real or fictitious, but whether you can believe in the possibility of those circumstances and imagine living as if they were your own. Actors, then, have to hone a very robust and purposeful form of daydreaming that enables them to see the world from a very particular *point of view* (or standpoint) that has been shaped by circumstances that may be very different from their own.

A character's point of view is unique to them. They've developed it over a lifetime of experiences via various social groups and experiences which have made them see the world around them in a particular way. If you think about wearing glasses with a strong colored tint, you can imagine the way the world looks suddenly new when you put them on. Suddenly, certain colors stand out, others disappear entirely. Looking at the world from a character's particular standpoint, the world you once saw will look different because their experiences have tinted their glasses differently. Actors can fuel their imaginative perspective adopting best with a variety of rich and specific details about the character and the world they inhabit.

This imaginative perspective adopting must take standpoint into consideration. While there have been some tensions amongst scholars about the perceived value or limitations of standpoint theory, it is important to understand two key ideas that arguably all standpoint theorists can agree upon. Alison Wylie, professor of philosophy and anthropology, presents these ideas as:

> First, standpoint theory must not presuppose an essentialist definition of the social categories or collectivities in terms of which epistemically relevant standpoints are characterized.
>
> Second, it must not be alighted with a thesis of automatic epistemic privilege—standpoint theorists cannot claim that those who occupy particular standpoints (usually subdominant, oppressed, marginal standpoints) automatically know more, or know better, by virtue of their social, political location. (28)

In other words, as noted earlier in this chapter, standpoint reminds us we cannot essentialize a social trait or cultural identity by saying things like "all women" or "all high school dropouts" as if everyone who connects to this identity has the exact same experience or understanding of the world. Likewise, standpoint theory reminds us that there isn't privileged knowledge based on our identities, moving us away from such broad ideas as "women's intuition" or "urban street smarts." While we use our imaginations to understand the world of the play, we must pay particular attention to not essentialize or afford privileged knowledge or awareness due to a social or political location in our analysis, and in particular how we unpack empathy and "if" in analysis.

No matter who the character is, imaginative perspective taking requires considerable creative work to accomplish. Even central characters driving the action of the plot are initially drawn only with as much detail as the script allows room for. Unlike a novel, a play unfolds over a set and comparatively brief amount of time (the length of the performance) in which a great deal must happen, and we often don't have direct access to the inner workings of a character's mind in important moments, so details may be slim.

This difficulty is even more pronounced for characters who appear less frequently or with whom the play does not actively try to get the audience to sympathize. **Antagonists,** in particular, may be difficult to create an empathetic link to because they are both less likely to have a richly detailed life provided by the script and are more likely to have motivations (as well as ideas and actions) that the audience is less sympathetic to. These characters probably don't think of themselves simply as villains motivated by malice and a proclivity toward evil. Most people are the heroes of their own stories, so developing a strong empathetic connection to such a character may require you to see actions and ideas that you might normally find abhorrent instead as justified if not heroic from your character's point of view.

Whether the character is easy to empathize with by design or not, an actor who is going to use empathy as a channel into their character needs to find a way to connect to the details of the character's life and take on that character's circumstances as if those circumstances are their own. This can help an actor add dimension and credibility to a character that might otherwise run the risk of being flat, insubstantial, or stereotypical. It also facilitates an actor feeling and behaving as their character would in the moment of performance.

Exercise 2.3: Cooling Down

The following two exercises are meant to go together, but Cooling Down can happen anytime you need it.

Actors generally acknowledge the value of warming up their body, voice, and mind before getting to work. Less often do they think of cooling down afterward, but taking the time to do so can provide a valuable final transition that allows you to separate from what can be physically and emotionally taxing work. Even when the work is joyful, it is worth taking the time to set the fictional aside and re-orient back to your life.

The deep imaginative work done for character analysis in this and following chapters may prove to be something worth cooling down afterward, whether or not you find it as strenuous as performing. There are many ways to cool down; you may even have something that works for you already. If not, here's something to try:

- Sit in a relaxed, upright position, or (usually better) lay down with plenty of space around you.
- If you are sitting, let your head float upward as if it is a balloon gently tugging your spine upward.
- If you lay down, lay on your back with your arms a little way out from your sides.
- Breathe deeply letting your diaphragm expand, and visualizing the breath sinking down to the level of your sacrum (below your belly button, about your tailbone).

- You may want to stretch or otherwise release unnecessary tension as you notice it.
- Visualize that with every breath, the creative work you've done, whether pleasant or not, works its way from within you to the surface of your skin like a sheen of sweat on a hot summer day.
- As it does so, you may simply take note of things that affected you without devoting too much thought to analyzing why.
- Little by little and as you continue deep breaths, let the work evaporate from your skin.
- Remind yourself that you are you, and the creative work you did isn't gone, but you don't need it now. You are just letting it go.
- Set the work adrift with your breath, knowing that you can recall it another time.
- Write down anything that felt important.

Again, this or any cool down routine can be used whenever you need to create a separation between your work and your life outside of that work. Try it again after the next exercise.

A Quick Note to Prepare for the Next Exercise

Before we start the next exercise, try answering the following as yourself, from your own standpoint. Freewrite without assuming you need to share or explain yourself to anyone else.

The world should be... (6–10 sentences)
Because... (6–10 sentences)

As mentioned earlier, the stories we tell and perform are full of characters for whom empathy won't come easily for a range of reasons. Some of these characters are difficult because their motivations are vague, some because they repulse us, some because they make choices we feel we would never make. Deliberately trying to create empathy for such a character can help deepen your analysis of them, and ultimately also help you perform them because you must seek to understand them if you are to make an empathetic connection. The following exercise aims to move you in that direction.

Exercise 2.4: Difficult Empathy

Part One

For this section, try an antagonist who is vaguely defined, just there to give the hero someone to clash with. The character could be from a play, although characters already established in popular culture may come more readily to mind.

Have a character in mind? Now try to understand their motivations by examining their words and their actions in particular. Do they repeat phrases? Do they use related words that you could put beneath the umbrella of "order," "power," "justice," or some other category? Do the actions they take or the ways they behave reveal something about how they believe the world *should* be? Make notes about these.

Now, just try writing a few sentences from their perspective. Write without thinking too much or editing for someone else's eyes:

The world should be... (3–5 sentences)
Because... (3–5 sentences)
I want... (1 sentence)
Because... (1 sentence)

Can you find any common ground, however small it may be, with this character? Do you agree that the world should be *just* even if you don't agree about what that *justice* looks like? Ordered, though you wouldn't take their actions to make it so? Free? Beautiful?

If you can find any common ground at all, that's the place to begin. If not, keep looking because you'll turn something up eventually. Even outlandish villains with extreme plans for the fate of the universe usually have a root desire that is relatable, like an overblown desire to create security or a skewed quest for justice that turns into revenge. From that meeting point between you and the character, you can build connections.

Part Two

This time try a character who is more well-defined, but who you don't easily relate to because their ideas are repulsive, their actions seem wrong, or what they want from the world is antithetical to what you want. For the purpose of this exercise, you might select a character from anywhere in all of fiction if it helps (movies, books, TV shows, as well as plays). If you already have a play that you are analyzing, try this exercise with a character whose standpoint is hard to immediately relate to.

Again, look at their language and their actions to see what those things reveal about who they are, what they want, and how they feel the world should be. After your notes are well underway, answer from their standpoint:

The world should be... (3–5 sentences)
Because... (3–5 sentences)
I want... (1 sentence)
Because... (1 sentence)

Then, take it further by answering some of the questions that have formed your emotional inventory in Exercise 2.1. Those prompts have been designed to help you define who and what you care about as well as what might provoke joy, anger, fear, sorrow, and wonder in you. What can the script tell you about the same emotions for this character? If the script neither outright says nor hints at an answer, what can you imagine seems justifiable based on what the script tells you?

The character may lead you to difficult conclusions because, for example, their fears are bigoted, or their joys make your skin crawl. That doesn't mean imagining your way into that point of view changes you or that you should be ashamed for being able to create an imaginative link to the character. These characters only have the power we lend them, and that can be rescinded at any time, so embrace your creative capacity in pursuing this difficult character and give yourself credit for the courage it takes to honestly try to foster empathy for someone who repulses you so much. Then, cool down.

Once you've established a suitable base for this character, try to find connections. Again, your definitions for right and wrong, freedom, order, love, or justice may be quite different, but at the core, you probably believe commonly in some things.

Next, identify who is important to the character. Who do they love? Who do they define themselves against? Then, see if you can make imaginative connections here, too. Do they feel protective of someone similarly to you? Do he long for someone in a way that you would if someone in your life was gone? It may be as simple as noticing that this character feels betrayed by someone they love, and you could understand how it would hurt if you were betrayed by someone you cared about.

The more you explore the common ground or the parallels between you and the character, the more easily you'll be able to imaginatively take on their circumstances. From this base, connections will grow and multiply, the more attention you give them. Future exercises will provide a template for doing just that.

Empathy and Understanding

Though empathy is enabled in part by understanding, understanding does not require empathy. For some who use this text, understanding may be the only goal. The depth of understanding created by at least trying to empathize and trying to take a look at the world through the character's eyes is still of tremendous benefit even if the full emotional experience never materializes. Imagining the life of someone else, particularly of someone you don't readily empathize with, helps you to humanize them in all their complexity. Once they have that level of dimension in your mind, they are a lot harder to simply dismiss because their worldview or standpoint doesn't neatly align with your own.

It is important to remember that the social groups referenced in standpoint theory are built from hierarchical structures rather than by the groups themselves. Patricia Hills Collins reminds us "Race, gender, social class, ethnicity, age, and sexuality are not descriptive categories of identity applied to individuals. Instead, these elements of social structure emerge as fundamental devices that foster inequality resulting in groups" (248). Ultimately, Hill Collins argues that common location within power structures is what creates groups rather than collective individuals. As we do the creative work of imagining the world of our characters, it is important to think about how are we maintaining hierarchical power structures by creating groups out of the "other?" We must also remember that being a member of a single social group does not imply that there is an overriding and all-encompassing group experience. Kristin Intemann reinforces this by stating, "Individuals from different social locations have, to some extent, different experiences" (785). As we imagine the lives of our characters, we must remember that how we experience the world through our own social groups and identity characteristics influences what options we allow ourselves to imagine for our characters. Our own self-awareness of our personal standpoint means we can be more open to imagine the "if" for our characters.

If

If is a tiny word with big implications. It signals a shift, diverting the flow of thoughts from *what is* into *what is not, but could be*. It takes us from this world into a world of parallel possibilities, alternatives to our current reality, hypotheticals. Stanislavski describes it as a password initiating the creative act, a lever that lifts an actor into their creative realm, and a magical prism allowing us to see a hypothetical world and react to it differently than we would our own (48–50). *If*, in this sense, isn't an invitation to let a delusion edge out reality, but to lay over the top of our accustomed reality a different perspective constructed from the imagined circumstances.

Children play naturally with unspoken *ifs*, turning the raw material of reality around them into the stuff of adventures, recasting themselves and those around them with new personas. They don't hallucinate lava engulfing the living room floor; they simply accept the premise, the "what if," and change their behavior accordingly. This ability doesn't leave us, though most of us see it diminish with disuse as we get older. So, it may take work to rekindle that vivid imagination and the willingness to accept the possibility of a fantasy as reality.

Stanislavski divided "ifs" between simple (single-story) ifs that could provoke an instantaneous response as if by magic and complex (multi-story) ifs that layered multiple hypotheticals on top of one another to add ever-increasing detail to the imagined reality (49–50). A *simple if* aims to get an actor to accept a suggestion that changes one small but significant element of reality. That change stimulates them to immediately adapt their behavior to it.

If we were to suggest the *simple if* to you that the cover of this book (or the device on which you are reading) has suddenly caught fire, and you accepted that imaginative stimulus, you might react in a number of ways. You may throw it to the floor, try to smother it, pour water over it, or call for help. These *ifs* are the "magic" ifs because they don't require thought from the actor. Instead, they happen immediately as a natural response to a suggestion. They tap into the established reaction to a stimulus that the actor already knows or has no trouble imagining. It requires very little thought to react to a sudden burst of flames in your hands. It just requires a willingness on your part to believe and the freedom to behave as you would if it were true.

If these simple ifs are magic, then the magic is that of transformation, allowing you to turn one object into another or otherwise giving it qualities it does not already have. They make carved styrofoam as heavy as a rock, they give tepid iced tea a bite like whiskey, and they sharpen a fine edge onto a dull prop sword. In so doing, they invite an actor to transform along with them, behaving as though the simple "what if" changes them, too.

In essence, this dual transformation is how Stanislavski envisions simple and complex *ifs* working. The actor accepts a hypothetical reality and allows that "what if" to change the way they view the world and act within it, living out the character's circumstances for the length of a performance. So, *complex ifs* have the same aim in mind, but do not rely solely on the immediate reaction of a simple hypothetical. They may require more thought such as following a logical sequencing of cause and effect along the lines of, "if X is true, then Y is also true, and as a result I may behave in Z way." Otherwise, they may rely on a confluence of multiple *ifs* to generate an effect.

Take, for example, the seemingly simple hypothetical, *what if you entered a café full of people and you went looking for a place to sit*. If you take on this hypothetical alone, you'd understandably behave more or less as yourself in carrying out that action. But, if you added complexity to the hypothetical as in, *what if you entered a café full of people and went looking for a place to sit, and what if you needed a quiet spot so you could write a personal email, and what if you were in a hurry because the contents are urgent?* Suddenly you may find your behavior changes considerably, choosing more carefully your spot, rushing to grab an open seat with space around it, ducking the eyes of the people at the counter so you won't feel like you have to order something first. The behavior would be considerably different if you added instead, ... *and what if you're new in town and want to meet people, and what if you've never ordered anything at a café like this before, and what if people have always complimented you on your smile, and what if people identify you as belonging to a social group that does not appear to be represented in this café?*

A series of related *ifs* (complex ifs) can set up the parameters for a scene and encourage behaviors without necessarily choreographing them. The *ifs* aren't there to dictate emotional reactions either. Instead, they set up the conditions for actions, allowing emotion to flow from the combination of the character's inner life (thoughts) and their outer behaviors (actions). Emotion, then, is something of a byproduct of fully accepting these *ifs*. It is a desirable result, of course, but feelings are not sought directly. Stanislavski also felt this way about suggesting *ifs* to spur an actor's imagination, saying that they should provoke an actor, but not force an emotional reaction on them (51).

Exercise 2.5: What if Café

This exercise can be done on paper or on its feet with other actors. The difference is that unanticipated discoveries usually happen when you enact something (especially with others). Working it out on paper, however, can alleviate the pressure of performance, which may be better for your personal creative flow. If you are approaching this exercise as a director, consider trying the exercise both from within (acting it out) and from the outside by guiding actors through the scenario and suggesting behaviors and changes throughout.

Imagine yourself in a café or set one up with multiple seating possibilities (chairs near people and separate, in corners and toward the center). Include a place to order. People are talking quietly in small groups, some are sitting alone, and there isn't a wait at the counter. Soft music is playing.

Now, follow the simple directions at whatever pace feels appropriate—you will order at some point, you will take a seat while you wait for your order to arrive, and you will receive a text on your phone that will prompt you to leave before your order comes. Then, layer a few ifs from below on top of that skeletal frame, either enacting them or thinking them through and writing down possible behaviors and actions. You might start by taking just one, but eventually try at least three operating at once. Let your focus be on actions and very minimally on speaking:

- *What if you are here to meet someone and you want to make a good impression?*
- *What if you aren't sure if you have enough money for your order and pay day is a few days away?*
- *What if you came in because you felt you were being followed?*
- *What if you're wearing your favorite outfit?*
- *What if you are insecure about your new haircut?*
- *What if no one in the café looks like you?*
- *What if your favorite song starts playing? Or you hate this music?*
- *What if the air conditioning is on way too high? Or broken?*
- *What if you came here to people watch but don't want anyone to notice?*
- *What if you recently broke up with someone and you used to come here together?*
- *What if your shoes don't quite fit right? Or some other part of your outfit?*
- *What if you ran here?*
- *What if you heard someone say they are from the same hometown as you?*
- *What if it was raining outside? Snowing?*
- *What if you don't speak the same language as everyone else?*
- *What if you recognize someone but can't place them? What if that's exciting? Unsettling?*
- *What if you are treating yourself after landing a new job? What if you just lost your job?*
- *What if this is your last day in town? What if that's great news? Or hard?*

Write down anything you discover or anything that feels important.

Ifs and Empathy

In a play, c*omplex ifs* like those in the exercise above build up over time as you continue analyzing the text and rehearse. They accrue from the details discovered about the world of the play and from constructing the character's unique standpoint within that world. They get richer as you collaborate with other actors. A director and designers add more specifics still.

Eventually, these details form the total illusion of the performance itself, an enveloping *if* that the actor accepts as a hypothetical reality to inhabit and react to from within the character's standpoint. As we will explore in Chapter 3, these *ifs* flow out of the *given circumstances*, the facts of the play, established not only by the play's text itself but also by the input of your artistic colleagues throughout the rehearsal process.

These hypotheticals are a way of very purposely engaging your empathy for a character. As you learn the facts of their past, their current circumstances, their desires, and their unique standpoint, you also develop the understanding that is vital for empathy. You can use this understanding to ask, "If these circumstances were my own, how would I react? What would I think? How would I see the world?" Then, you have the perspective to act as they would. And, with openness and a willingness to accept these circumstances as your own, you hope that you will begin to feel as they would, too.

For an actor, empathy's primary purpose is to help you act as the character would if their circumstances were your own. With rehearsal, this reaction to circumstances may come automatically. For some, it may take deliberate thought prior to rehearsal, pages and pages of "if, then" to consider. In either case, it is useful to map actions out, as we will explore in later chapters, even if those actions adjust in the moment of performance. You need a plan, as well as a willingness to accept that plans change when they meet reality.

Again, emotions are the byproduct of this deep imaginative process and the actions you take in response to your imaginings. You have some control over the conditions to make that emotion possible, but rarely do you have much control over the emotions themselves. In a sense, pursuing emotion in a scene is very much like planting a seed; you can set up the conditions the plant needs in order to grow by choosing good soil, a spot with plenty of sun, and watering carefully. In the end, however, you cannot control the plant itself. And, in the case of emotions, you may think you've planted an orange tree only to see it bears cherries. Given this uncertainty, it is better for an actor to focus on the *ifs* and the actions, letting the emotions take care of themselves.

Exercise 2.6: If, Then

In Exercise 2.1, you have begun an emotional inventory and in the next section, we'll start to use that collected self-knowledge to help you connect your life with the character's life. This exercise will lay a foundation for that work by connecting that inventory to hypotheticals.

Imagine that your task is simply to encourage an emotion in yourself— joy, fear, anger, love, wonder, or sadness. Select one emotion and write it at the top of a sheet of paper. Next, look at your emotional inventory and find the things about yourself that resonate with that emotion and list them below. If new ideas emerge, add them too. These are the raw material from which you can create a hypothetical that encourages the emotion at the top.

Now, create a simple "if, then" scenario based on that raw material. "If this person I care about betrayed me, then how would I react? What might I do?" Or "If I got the chance to do this exciting activity with that person who makes me happy, then what would I do?" You might use only one thing, you might combine several, or an entirely new idea might come to you.

Set a timer between 5 and 10 minutes. From that initial "if, then," let a fictional story evolve, writing as if it has recently happened to you (or is happening now) and you are speaking your mind. Write without editing or stopping. Don't worry about ever sharing it with someone else, that's up to you to decide later. Your task is only to get ideas out quickly. Return to the original "if, then" as needed and start new branches out from that initial hypothetical.

Once the timer goes off, cool down. Repeat this activity as often as you like. Know that new ideas may surface, so revisiting the same scenario can still be fruitful. In essence, this exercise is meant to help you imaginatively spark an emotion you don't currently feel. If the story is believable to you and you can accept that hypothetical as reality (at least temporarily), then some measure of that emotion may grow within you.

You can modify the exercise to ask a question that would relate to an action more than an emotion if need be. For example, "What would it take for me to steal?" Or "What would it take for me to dance around the room and make a fool of myself?" Once you know the question you want answered, use your emotional inventory to create an "if, then" that answers that question. "If..., then I would need to steal," and "if..., then I'd want to dance."

When you try to relate to a character (their emotions, their actions), creating a hypothetical which might spark emotions and actions in you that are the same or similar to the characters can help you to bridge that distance. Without hypotheticals, understanding and empathizing with a character can be more difficult. With them, you learn that certain circumstances can shape you to do and feel things that you might not expect.

The Character in the Actor

Using *if* to engage your empathy and discover actions, you not only find the character, but you find yourself within the character. Rather than being a mask or a coat to be put on and removed, in this style of acting, the character emerges from within an actor, often amplifying aspects of their existing personality while muting others. The character may be a contorted, funhouse mirror version of an actor, but that actor is nevertheless the reflection's origin. This can be unsettling, particularly if the character is someone you'd rather think of as very different and separate from yourself. All the more reason to develop a cool down routine in order to re-orient you to the world.

One approach for drawing the character out of you is finding ways that their ideas or circumstances correspond to your own, clearly drawing parallels between them and you. Consider, for example, a character that has a deep passion for astronomy which they must express regularly, as Henrietta does in Lauren Gunderson's *Silent Sky*. Even if you are fascinated by astronomy yourself, unless your passion for it blazes like Henrietta's, you'll need to find something analogous for yourself.

So, you can ask yourself what excites you the way astronomy excites Henrietta. The simple act of drawing such a parallel can spark your imagination. "The way Henrietta feels about astronomy is like the way I feel about..." Once that's established, the *ifs* can begin, this time as correlating the character's life to your own. "If I got the opportunity to pursue my passion the way Henrietta gets to invited to pursue hers in the first scene, then what might I do?" And, "If I was tantalizingly close to pursuing that passion only to suddenly be kept from it, then how might I react?"

This search for analogies is why Exercise 2.1 (and, for that matter, a sustained attempt to know yourself in general) is important. A character's circumstances, their social groups, their privileges, their ideas, and their actions can seem abstract if you can't find a way to relate to them. Even an imperfect analogy can bridge the distance between the abstract and the concrete, facilitating your empathy and leading you to actions. So, you benefit from being familiar with one half of this equation before you start to address the other, from being familiar with *you*.

These parallels can help you erode barriers like "I don't understand why my character would do this," or "I can't connect to my character because I would never do that." A character's actions can often seem strange to us. Characters may even surprise themselves by taking actions they wouldn't expect themselves to ever take. Generally, though, those actions come as a consequence of their circumstances, even if it is not always a *logical* response to those circumstances. Paralleling these causes and effects with ones of your own, real or imagined, can help make sense of that reaction because you've likened it to an imaginative experience of your own.

Exercise 2.7: If, Then with Characters

Here, you will revisit the exercise established in Exercise 2.5, but now you need a character. If you are already working on a play, use a character from it. If you are analyzing as a director or a designer, you might repeat this exercise for every character you are trying to learn more about.

Find some action or emotion of the character which you want to relate to. Use it to create a specific hypothetical for yourself that would generate a similar emotion or provoke a similar action in you. Remember to start with an initial "if, then" sentence from which to let a scenario grow. For example, "If (blank) happened to me, then I would be thrilled." or "If (blank) happened to me, then I would be angry."

Once you have it, freewrite for 5–10 minutes. Return to the initial "if, then" as often as needed. Once you finish, cool down.

I Contain Multitudes

Given time to imagine ourselves into similar circumstances as those of the character—using hypotheticals drawn from the social groups, personal identities, and histories of our lives—we can more readily empathize with characters. This builds off of Stanislavski's conception of *ifs*, which focused more on directly taking on the character's circumstances as if they are your own. This perspective taking remains at the heart of the previous sections of this chapter, but here we want to acknowledge that this is not always a simple substitution to make.

The theory posited through Exercises 2.5 and 2.6 is that given the right circumstances, we are all capable of actions and emotions that might surprise us. Particular circumstances shape particular outcomes and so the specific details of our past and present circumstances have a tremendous influence on who we are now. So, our actions and emotions (and, indeed, much of our identity) are the product of our socio-cultural context as much as they are of our inner selves. We are influenced by our standpoint, our life experiences, the way the world views us, the way we grew up, learned, and matured. But, we are also shaped by where we live, what social groups we belong to, who was around us, and millions of small things we absorbed from our immediate surroundings. Our actions and our emotions are shaped by our ideals, our aspirations, and biases. Indeed, we are so completely shaped by our circumstances and social location that changing them necessarily changes us. This will be a repeated refrain in the next few chapters. We are all full of different potentials, different selves that could emerge given the right combination of circumstances. Accepting that possibility should make it easier to see another's very different perspective and to imagine ourselves into someone else's shoes.

Further Reading

Collins, Patricia Hill. "Comment on Hekman's 'Truth and Method: Feminist Standpoint Theory Revisited': Where's the Power?" *The Feminist Standpoint Theory Reader: Intellectual and Political Controversies*, edited by Sandra Harding, New York: Routledge, 2004, 247–253.

Harding, Sandra. "Introduction: Standpoint Theory as a Site of Political, Philosophic, and Scientific Debate." *The Feminist Standpoint Theory Reader: Intellectual and Political Controversies*, edited by Sandra Harding, New York: Routledge, 2004, 1–16.

Heckman, Susan. "Truth and Method: Feminist Standpoint Theory Revisited." *The Feminist Standpoint Theory Reader: Intellectual and Political Controversies,* edited by Sandra Harding, New York: Routledge, 2004, 225–241.

Intemann, Kristen. "25 Years of Feminist Empiricism and Standpoint Theory: Where Are We Now?" *Hypatia: A Journal of Feminist Philosophy*, vol. 25, no. 4, 2010, pp.778–796.

Teding van Berkhout and Emily & John Malouff. "The Efficacy of Empathy Training: A Meta-Analysis of Randomized Controlled Trials." *Journal of Counseling Psychology*, vol. 63, no 10, . 2015.

Wylie, Alison. "Why Standpoint Matters." *Science and Other Cultures: Issues in Philosophies of Science and Technology,* edited by Robert Figueroa and Sandra Harding, New York: Routledge, 2003.

Quick Definitions

Antagonist: A person who is working actively against someone or something.

Empathy: Adopting someone else's perspective, a process of inserting yourself into another's shoes so fully that you can both understand them and feel as they do.

Essentialism: The belief that a set of characteristics naturally make someone what they are.

If: What is not, but could be

Magic if: Allowing us to see a hypothetical world and react to it differently than we would our own

Social location: Position in social or cultural groups

Standpoint theory: One's social position and group associations impact how the world sees you and how you see the world.

Sympathy: Affected by the emotions and situations of another

Chapter 3

Place Theory and Given Circumstances

This chapter explores the depth of meaning in place and how our relationships to geographical places, the people who dwell there, and the cultural norms embraced by that place impact our understanding of the world. The details offered in given circumstances are often detailed in the world or places of the play.

"There's no place like home."

Home is a word imbued with meaning for each and every one of us. It could mean a place of comfort and joy, pain and embarrassment, or some recipe of both. These well-known words from the 1939 film *The Wizard of Oz* indicate the complexity of place attachment. Dorothy's desire to go "home" most obviously indicates a wish to return to a geographical place (a farmhouse in Kansas instead of the technicolor world of Oz), to familiar people (Auntie Em and Uncle Henry rather than witches, wizards, and talking scarecrows), and to a context where she understands expectations and cultural norms (greetings of hello and a wave rather than songs of welcome by small people in brightly colored clothes or princesses in sparkling tiaras). Examining place, in all of its complexities, is an important element of understanding the world of our characters as well as our own.

Context

Context is key to unlocking a character. Knowing a character's circumstances in specific detail brings their world to life, making them far easier to comprehend and perform. Without a clear sense of a character's circumstances, their motivations may seem strange and the actions that they take remain difficult to understand. When struggling with a character, some actors will say that they are having difficulty with their character because "I would never do what they do in this play." Building on the "magic if" of Chapter 2, it may be true, but it also may be that your actions would surprise you *if* your circumstances were different. Under specific circumstances, we are all capable of doing things we might not otherwise expect from ourselves.

A character's circumstances are the set of lived facts that shape them and their actions. These facts situate the character in time, place, and culture. They construct the world through which the character currently moves and the influences that have shaped the character's particular point of view leading up to the events of the play. Knowing these details brings the character's world to light and the way they view or react to that world into focus. Without establishing them—without context—a character is far more difficult to understand, let alone empathize with.

In Stanislavski's phrasing, the *given circumstances* are the set of facts received by the actor primarily from the playwright (53). They create the character's world with needed details like *who* is this character? *Where* are they now and *when* is now? These given circumstances, in addition to those presented by the director and other members of the production team, Stanislavski admits, are often insufficient to create a complete and engaging fantasy life. They must be further developed by the actor's research and imagination in order to populate the world of the play with specific detail (Stanislavski 62–71). Doing so helps to set off the deep empathetic process that allows an actor to inhabit a role.

So, these details must be known, imagined, and accepted as the actor's imagined reality.

What's more, these details should also be as specific as possible. We live our lives in particular circumstances, even if we are not always fully cognizant of those circumstances. If we were to set you on an empty stage and ask you to imagine that you are outside, that's simply far too general to create much from. Are you outside on a bright, sunny day? A moonless night? And what kind of outside are we talking about? Out on an unfamiliar city street? On a deserted beach with a strong wind blowing in? In the depths of a mosquito filled bog? Each change in circumstances affects the imaginary world and how you will react to it. The richer the detail, the more likely you are able to invest in the imaginary circumstances. Generalities simply can't spark enough creativity.

Understanding the place of the character is important and, as noted in the *Wizard of Oz* example, more complex than simply a location. Maria Lewicka, psychologist and place theorist, asserts that the strength of our relationship to place is based on several factors, including "the places themselves (their scale, size, physical and social characteristics) and people (their social and economic status, residence length and mobility, age, sense of security, social relations in the place, value system, etc.)" (209). How we feel about a place stems from a complex set of thoughts and relationships that link many layers of the self together. As you move through this chapter teasing out how to understand place for yourself and your character, keep Lewicka's definition of place in mind.

We'll start with an active exercise intended to bring your attention to the way in which the details of one's immediate surroundings shape behavior and attitude. The exercise combines imagined physical and mental stimuli. It should serve as a reminder that at any point in a play, characters are immersed in a world of stimulation that prompts reactions in the body, the memory, the intellect, and their emotions.

Exercise 3.1: A Journey in the Imagination

This exercise invites you to inhabit imaginary circumstances on your feet. It helps to do the exercise with at least one other person reading the prompts below while any others move through the space, visualize, and react to those prompts. It also helps for those moving to go into the exercise without knowing what is coming, but it isn't necessary.

Going forward, remember that there is no need to perform for one another if you are in a group. Simply accept the prompts as an imagined reality you are going to walk through, then physicalize your response to the prompts. In responding, imagine with all your senses. There will be things to see, hear, touch, taste, and smell. These might come directly from the prompts, or they may be sparked in your imagination by some association you make with the prompts. Allow yourself to build off of each prompt in simple ways.

You'll want room to move. Start with actors walking about the space. Watch out for walking around and around in a circle; this pattern isn't necessary or best. Be aware of impulses to turn, change direction, stop, and to move again from a stop. Try moving to fill open spaces as they occur and maintaining a sense that you need to keep moving forward.

Warm Up to the Journey

- Warm up to the Journey by simply walking about the space as yourself, but yourself on a good day. Maybe you were recently engaging in a conversation in which you made some really good points. Maybe a friend gave you a compliment that made you feel appreciated. Maybe you just really like the way you looked in the mirror today. Whatever it is, you're having a good day.
  - Physicalize your reactions. Imagine in detail. Move through and past simple interpretations and embrace unexpected reactions.
  - See friendly faces all around you. Feel good weather. Smell good cooking in the air. Hear music, or birds, or laughter.

- Notice how your attitude—physical and mental—changes in this mindset. Notice how you respond to sensations. How are you walking? How are you carrying yourself? What are your eyes doing? Your mouth? Your arms and legs? How does it feel to walk about this way?
- Now, take that good day away and replace it with a bad one. Maybe you have embarrassed yourself in front of people you respect. Maybe your friends have been ditching you lately. Maybe you just don't feel like you fit into your surroundings.
  - Physicalize your reactions. Imagine in detail. As above, move past simple interpretations to more nuanced or surprising reactions.
  - See condescending grimaces all around you, or eyes that are making you feel unwelcome. Sense bad weather that you didn't dress well for. Let a foul stench creep up on you. Hear harsh sounds, unfriendly shouting, or some other unpleasant drone.
  - Notice changes in your physical and mental attitude. What's different? What are the sensations doing to you this time?
- Let that all go and cool down with activities mentioned in Chapter 2.

As you try the full exercise, remember to be checking in with yourself throughout. Notice reactions that you have to the stimuli in the prompts throughout. These stimuli of geographic place, familiar denizens of that place, and the social or cultural customs of that place all factor into how you respond and react. For example, if you are from an urban area where noise is common, the prompt of unfriendly shouting may feel more comfortable than it does to someone from an isolated rural area. Even the simple "unfriendly shouting" grounds itself in place which we will build upon in the next exercise. If you're working with a prompter, that person can ask you to consider the sights, smells, sounds, feel, taste, and associations that come with each step. They can encourage those imagining the journey to consider what the prompt makes them feel, want, or want to do in response.

A Journey

At each step, ask "What changes?"; "What changes physically?"; "What changes about my attitude?"; "How do I feel?"; and "What does that make me want to do in response?". Physicalize your reactions and imagine in detail.

- Begin moving about the space again, just as yourself. Instead of being inside, imagine that you are outside. Imagine that you are in familiar surroundings, perhaps just outside the space you are in right now. The weather is good.
- As you walk, notice that your surroundings are increasingly unfamiliar to you. Notice that you don't recognize the places or faces you pass. The heat of the day builds.
- Come to an open space, away from signs of civilization. The heat builds. Your surroundings become increasingly arid. You feel lost and you haven't seen anyone else in some time.
- The heat builds, it feels like dangerous heat. Your surroundings have changed to someplace rocky and uneven. Perhaps there's sand. You grow increasingly thirsty.
- Water in the distance! Go to the water, see that it's clean and cool. Try drinking it. Run your hands through. Try playing in it, experience the cool relief after that dangerous heat.
- Come to the edge of the water, and let it change and expand in your imagination. Let it become the edge of a great body of water, one so big you cannot see the other shore. Warm sand stretches out under your feet. Feel the breeze, smell the salt air, listen to the waves and seabirds.
- Feel and respond to an urge to get in. Take your time so you can notice the changes from the first splash that covers your foot all the way up to chest deep.
- Imagine that you're able to continue walking along the ocean floor without concern for breathing. How does the resistance of the water feel? What are the

sights? How do things change as you get deeper and the waters grow darker?
- Start to re-emerge into shallower waters without yet breaking the surface. Then, imagine that whatever kept you breathing has suddenly stopped. Hurry to the surface. Break the water's surface and feel the deep relief of air returning to your lungs.
- Emerge from the water again on this far shore. This beach is cooler, and the sun is setting. The beach itself is rocky rather than sandy, the wind more forceful. Notice the differences.
- Let your clothes dry, as if by magic. Walk inland and notice that the temperature continues falling and the sun continues to drop closer to the horizon. The air is crisp, it carries the smell of pine and a coming snowfall. Quickly the snow begins to float down, accumulating enough to crunch beneath your feet.
- Not far off you see a small fire. Trudge through deep snow to it. Feel its warmth. There's a smell of burning wood and a gentle crackle. Night has truly fallen. You have a sense that you must keep moving. Leave the fire and step out into a moonlit night.
- As you walk, trees become more numerous and the sky is increasingly hidden by branches. Notice the sounds as you snap branches. Ducking and stepping over roots, you are forced to move differently through the woods. A smell pervades of rotting leaves. You hear animals that you cannot see.
- A sense that something is following you grows in your mind. You stop and can hear the noise of something large in the woods, not far behind. Try moving quietly and carefully away.
- It's no good, you have to run. Remember that there are still branches to duck, roots to step over. See ahead that there is light as the forest ends in a clearing. Break into a large meadow with the certainty that whatever was pursuing you won't follow you out of the woods.
- The sun has risen again, you see that the meadow is full of flowers and butterflies. Bees buzz past and the

Place Theory and Given Circumstances 67

air is full of pleasant aroma. The grass is tall, as you pass by it reaches your hands. There is a building up a small hill rising up before you. It's hard to make out at this distance, but with every step, it takes shape.

- Soon you'll reach a home. It will be perfect for you, whatever that means. Perfect might mean full of friends and family. That's great, but if that's so, then just imagine that everyone is out. Memories of them will linger and evidence of people may remain in things like discarded sweaters or music left playing. They just aren't here right now. Every step brings this home more into view until you are standing at the door, ready to open it.
- Swing the door open and pause at the threshold. Let sights and smells come to you that make you feel a sense of home. Perhaps a recently cooked meal lingers in the air, or familiar furniture. Move through the space and interact with the sights, sounds, smells, and textures of a perfect home. Let your imagination play.
- Turn and face a room that holds some object of delight—something that brings you delight. Interact with it in whatever way makes sense for this object.
- Leave that space and explore some more. Then, turn and face a room that holds an object of beauty—something that you find divine in its style or shape or color. Interact with this object in whatever way makes sense for it.
- Leave that space explore some more. Let the sense build that this is a home you share with someone who is important to you—perhaps even deeply loved. Let this person be completely imaginary and imagine a very specific relationship with them.
- Turn and face a room of shared joy—a room that holds memories of this other person and time spent with them. Interact with the memories in the room though this person is absent.
- Now, let your imagination reshape this same space as you get the sense that this person you once shared joy with is gone, and it is your fault. Re-experience this room and its memories with the knowledge that they are gone, and they won't return.

- Move through this once perfect place and experience it again with a new sense of loss. Find the object of beauty and see how things have changed as you interact with them. Find the object of delight and see how things have changed as you interact with them, too.
- As you walk through this home, let the sense build in you that it is too painful to live here anymore, and you must leave it. Take it in with all your senses, but with the sense that you are leaving. Take a moment at the threshold, again. This moment is a final goodbye to the home. Then, step back into the meadow.
- Walk away from this place and into the meadow. Without fully understanding why, realize that with every step a sense of hope builds in you. You have a sense of certainty that, while leaving, this life will be hard, something better awaits.
- Cool down.

After the Journey

Hopefully, this exercise serves as a vivid reminder of the direct impact our immediate circumstances and our past circumstances can have on our attitudes and actions. Sensory input from our environment causes immediate reactions in us. Our responses to places that cause discomfort or fear are just as important to acknowledge and assess. What is it particularly about those places that cause distrust? How are those places connected to our social or cultural groups (standpoint)? Since the environment and our attitude toward it provokes such strong responses, these should be accounted for in our characters. What are their current environmental circumstances? What's around them? What's stimulating their senses?

Place attachment theorists, Irwin Altman and Setha M. Low, encourage us to think of place in terms of affect. They assert that individuals develop attachment to places that "provide opportunities for privacy, personal displays, security, and serenity" (7). For many of us, our memories of the past can impact our relationship to places that evoke the security and safety that Altman and Low indicate. For some of us, the memories of past places can trigger emotions that evoke the absence of those feelings of serenity and peace. How you responded to the various 'places' in the previous exercises helps connect the individual experience to the relationships of place. For some, the outdoors and solitude may bring peace while the outdoors may cause distress and anxiety.

It can be easy to forget that the past can often be quite present for a character, and it is still significant and affecting them in the current moment. Memories have sensorial components that can suddenly seem very much in the room with us now. Characters may well experience this too, even if they do not explicitly say so. Memories and associations that a character may make from their environment function as a transparency laid over the top of the character's current experience of the world. Consider what feelings and memories may be attached to a room, another person, a few notes on the radio, a smell, or a taste.

Asking Questions

Let's say you're playing a character who enters an apartment. The stage directions supplied are along the lines of:

Enters. Takes a quick look around, then decides to sit down.

For now, it's as simple as that. Enter. Walk around the room. Sit. As it stands, there's not a lot of imaginary world to inhabit in this, so there's not a lot that would make this moment and this character particular rather than general.The only distinction might be if the character has never encountered an apartment. Beyond that, the character's life outside that door is blank. They've come from no place, they seem to be no one in particular, and where they are isn't very clear. That's because the circumstances of this small unit of action remain unknown or undetermined.

Your circumstances are important because they change your behavior as you enter. Your entrance changes dramatically depending, for example, on where you came from moments ago. If you excitedly run up several flights of stairs to get here, you'll enter differently than you would if you casually strolled down the hall from an apartment on the same floor, or whether your rode the elevator to the penthouse apartment. Whose space you're in now matters a great deal, too. You're likely to walk about the apartment differently if it is very familiar to you than you would if it was your first time, or if you entered expecting to see someone who isn't there as opposed to if you expected to be alone. Because these details shape the imaginary world you're entering and how you react to that world, they must be known. Asking questions helps you bring shape to this otherwise formless world and vague character.

Both the present moment and the thousands of moments that led the character here have bearing on a character and their actions. The character's desires for the future do too, but we'll save that for another chapter. The questions below should help you orient your character within their present circumstances and help you better situate their history. Not all questions will seem relevant at first, but keep an open mind. Remember these two things:

- You can't be sure which discovery will suddenly open a door into the character's world for you or bring it suddenly to life. Some actors are very surprised to find that one nugget they thought was irrelevant turned out to unlock far more than they would have first guessed. So, try to answer these questions without concerning yourself too much about the end result.
- Often, little details are meaningless on their own, but when combined with others, begin to show a pattern. This can be hard to see when you're up close, but once

Place Theory and Given Circumstances 71

those small points are established, you can step back and see a bigger picture resolve.

Finally, not all circumstances are simply given by the playwright or supplied later by the director or designers. In order to create a complete set of circumstances, actors have to combine a mixture of facts given by the playwright, facts derived from research, and facts deduced from their imaginations based on the first two. As you make your discoveries, it is important to keep track of where those facts come from, especially in the event that one fact contradicts another. It is important to know which of the following phrases would preface each circumstance:

The playwright says directly (through stage direction or a character's line)...

> I can deduce from hints in the script that...
> My research says directly...
> I can deduce from my research...
> I imagine based on the text that...
> I imagine based on my research that...

If a fact coming from your imagination contradicts a fact from your research or the play, then you must reconcile your imagination to those two. If a fact from your research contradicts the story, then honor the play's reality and the playwright's intentions. A playwright may well be giving you a character who does not fit the mold of their time or be using anachronisms purposefully in order to make some comment or connection between the play and the audience.

Your creative impulses do not always need to be completely disregarded when you run into contradictions either. For example, because of something in the text, you might imagine that your character was a raucous troublemaker in their youth only to find that you've overlooked a line where your character says they lived a very dull life up until this point. How will you reconcile your creative impulse to the fact expressed in the text? Are they lying? Are you simply wrong? You could simply adjust your creative impulse, of course. You could also trust that your creative impulse has merit too and reconcile it by imagining that while your character did lead a very dull life up to this point, they also had a yearning to break the rules which they simply suppressed everywhere but in their daydreams.

Exercise 3.2: Tracking Facts

You'll begin collecting facts over the course of this chapter. Don't forget to return to the Personal Glossary (exercises 1.3) as a starting point. Those facts will accumulate as you continue working on the play. It can become very easy for those facts to sprawl into disorganization. Take a moment here to create a "home base" for those facts. On the top of a blank page, write the title "Facts from the Playwright," and subtitle with whatever character you are working on. On this page, write down any facts directly stated by the playwright that are relevant and pertain to your character. These might be things a character says about themselves, statements made in stage directions, or things said by other characters.

Once you've established a list, identify gaps within the list that must be filled with research, with your own imagination, or some combination thereof. For example, the characters all reference the stock market crash, but you don't know what that is. Or the siblings in the play all reference a traumatic family dinner, but the playwright doesn't provide you with enough details to visualize it. With this list you will know what facts you need to uncover through research or by creatively filling in the gaps. You will also always be able to return to this list of facts as a touchstone, the foundational information against which you can check new discoveries for contradictions. Don't worry if some of the pages remain blank. We will be building on these ideas through the rest of the chapter. Be attentive to this list as you fill in the details of a character's life. When do contradictions pop up? How do you reconcile them to the playwright's text?

For the purposes of organization, you can use the list from earlier to title other pages:

I can deduce from hints in the script that...
I need to research...
My research says directly...
I can deduce from my research...
I imagine based on the text that...
I imagine based on my research that...

In this way, as details emerge you know where they came from and can better locate them again.

Questions

The upcoming questions in this section are phrased as questions to your character. Any time you analyze a character, you have the option of doing so from a third person vantage point or a first. For an actor, answering in the first person can help you to develop the character's voice, easing your ability to later enact and embody them. If you're better served by answering in the third person, do so.

These questions are thorough, but by no means all encompassing. You may find there are other questions to ask of a character. If so, ask away. More details could lead to an important discovery.

Let's start with questions that get at the character's identity. Who you are (as a character) and who the people around you are in relation to you is perhaps one of the most complex and urgent questions for an actor, so much so that further chapters will return to this question again and again. Remember, some of these questions can be answered by the text in one way or another. Others will require a combination of research and your own creativity. For now, try establishing some essential facts. Remember to use the categories established in exercise 3.2.

Present Circumstances

- What's your name? How would you introduce yourself?
- How old are you?
- Who are you in the eyes of the other people in the play? How do you relate to them?
- How would you describe your gender identity?
- How would you describe your racial identity?
- How would you describe your ethnic identity?
- How would you describe your economic situation and status?
- Do you have neurological characteristics that shape your identity?
- Do you have physical characteristics that shape your identity?
- Do you have an occupation?
- Do you have interests, ideals, or beliefs that significantly shape your sense of self?
- Are there other significant facets of your life that shape your identity (religion, for example)?
- What social groups do you belong to?

Formative Circumstances

- Who raised you? Who mentored you? Who have you considered family?
- What were the lasting lessons you took from these people?
- Who were your friends?
- Who did you emulate? Who did you try hard not to emulate? Do you emulate someone still? Why?
- What is a single, powerful moment from your childhood?
- How has your identity or your conception of your identity changed over time? Have there been significant moments in the evolution of your identity or your awareness of it?

Time and place also have a significant impact on a character. First off, the very immediate circumstances of a character's present have a direct influence on behavior and attitude. Consider how differently your character may behave if they are up at two in the morning in an emergency room than they might in the middle of the day, or how your character might occupy the furniture in the cozy familiarity of their own home compared to the uncertainty of the first visit to the home of someone they've only just gotten to know. In any given place, your character might find stimuli that alter their attitude and behavior. Does the smell of fresh bread waft into the room? Is there a piece of decor that your character finds disgusting or unsettling on the walls? Is winter seeping in from the windows? Or a blazing, midsummer sun? Any of these could change the way a character inhabits a place, even if they aren't always conscious of the change in their behavior.

Secondly, more broad questions of "where" and "when" your character lives will nuance and complicate your character's concept of identity. Not all eras and geographic locations had, for example, a concept of race that was anything close to what has developed in the United States over the last 50, 200, or 400 years. One's gender and sexual identity are similarly formed by one's specific cultural moment and context. Putting on a corset for a historical production is a very forceful reminder of the roles and expectations of women in many centuries and countries. The norms of a region and an era can shift rapidly even within ten years or ten blocks, so this is another place for you to seek specificity.

Now let's explore present and formative circumstances with a specific focus on time and place, again adding to the categories established in exercise 3.2.

Present Circumstances Time/Place Specific

- What time is it?
- What day of the week is it?
- What time of year is it? What season is it?

- What year is it?
- How would you describe the times you live in?
- Where are you (your immediate surroundings)?
- How would you describe your immediate surroundings?
- How are your senses stimulated in your current environment? Sight? Smell? Sound? Taste? Touch?
- Where are you when you think about the surrounding geography? Region? City? 10-mile radius?
- What kind of dwelling do you live in? In what country do you live?

Formative Circumstances Time/Place Specific

- When were you born?
- Where were you born?
- Where did you live growing up?
- How would you describe the changes in your society in the last ten or so years?
- Were there moments of significant social change in or around your lifetime?
- Do you live near the place of your birth and/or the place where you were raised? Has that made a difference for you?
- How have your surroundings changed in the last ten or so years?

As you take into account the answers to these questions, keep in mind the way power and privilege work in tandem with our understanding of place. Eve Tuck and Marcia McKenzie call upon the work of several scholars across a variety of disciplines to highlight the ways place is "experienced differently based on culture, geography, gender, race, sexuality, age, or other identifications and experiences; and to understand how these disparate realities determine not only how place is experienced but also how it is understood and practiced in turn" (36). In addition to their social groups as discussed in Chapter 2, characters are also a product of their time and place. Rarely can we escape the influences of our cultural moment, though some are inevitably going to be outliers in their time. Is this your character? Do they think in ways that are unconventional for their time? Do they fit in with the neighbors on their street? Once you've established a sense of the dominant culture your character lives within, that is the culture that dictates norms and expectations, it's worth asking how well they fit in to their time and place. This may lead you away from some of these more concrete details into another category of question—what does your character know or believe about the world? Before we follow that question, stop to take an inventory of what you know, what you need to find out.

Exercise 3.3: Discovering the Details

Once you've answered the above questions, you should have a fairly clear understanding of the character and their circumstances starting to emerge. You may also find that there are questions for which you have only partial answers, so the details aren't as clear as they could be. A good place to start is your "I need to research..." page from exercise 3.2. You may know that you are playing Marie Antionette, but need to know how much (or little) privacy that meant as you walked through Versailles. You may know that your character's weekly pay is $76 a week, but do not have a sense of whether that is enough to make ends meet in 1950s Pittsburgh or not. Some questions are important enough that they require additional research to help you better imagine the circumstances. Take some time to catalog those questions here.

Now ask, "How can I get the answers that I need?" Consider the kind of research you are able to do that can help feed your imagination. Look for resources that could hold answers for you and list them beside each question. This research can help take you from a generalized imagination of the character's circumstances to a detailed imaginative world which you can inhabit. As you discover details, remember to track—what do I know from the playwright?

What do I know because of the research I've done? What do I imagine based on what I've deduced from the play or my research?

Tinted Glasses

Not everyone from the same place and time thinks the same way. Yes, they are influenced by the dominant culture of that time and place, but there are multiple influences on a character that subtly tinge their view of the world. Some of their views may correlate with aspects of their identity, so when searching for an answer to the following, remember that your character's lived experience can draw them to certain principles and understandings of the world.

Linking Stanislavski's concept of Given Circumstances with Place Attachment theory is important as you move through your character analysis. Altman and Low's foundational ideas about place can add depth to your analysis. They assert place can "provide a sense of daily and ongoing security and stimulation, with places and objects offering predictable facilities, opportunities to relax from formal roles, the chance to be creative and to control aspects of one's life" (10). Like Dorothy's "no place like home" mantra, our sense of self and safety are strengthened by understanding our place in the world. Pushing the connection to place further, Altman and Low indicate "place attachment may link people with friends, partners, children, and kin in an overt and visible fashion. It may bond people to others symbolically, providing reminders of childhood or earlier life, parents, friends, ancestors, and others. Furthermore, place attachments may link people to religion, nation, or culture by means of abstract symbols associated with places, values, and beliefs" (10). Our foundational ideas about the world are built upon how we understand our coonection to the people, places, and social situations around us. This web is deeply personal for every individual and character.

Again, building upon the categories established in 3.2, answer the following questions considering the complexities of place attachment.

Present Circumstances Place Attachment specific

- How would you summarize your worldview?
- Do you have a personal motto?
- Do you have a moral code Or a system of ethical beliefs?
- How would you describe your philosophy on life?
- What are the major cultural influences on you?
- Where is a place or location of comfort for you? Why is it comfortable?
- How is any of the above influencing your approach to your current circumstances? Your choices? Your actions?

Formative Circumstances Place Attachment specific

- What, if anything, were you brought up to believe about the world?
- From where did you derive a personal code or system of beliefs?
- What did this lead you to believe about morality, ethics, or philosophy?
- What have been the major cultural influences on you?
- What do you think of when you think of home? Is it a geographic location? Is it a dwelling? Is it the people within that dwelling?
- What have been the significant shifts in your worldview over the last ten or so years?

As you seek answers to these questions, you'll begin to see a very particular point of view emerge, the character's unique view as you understand it. This is the perspective from which they view their circumstances—their time, their immediate surroundings, the people with whom they interact. You may find in your character someone either very much in step with their time or a step outside of it. You may find a character who sees social ills that others look past. You may find a character thriving in the status quo. You may find that your character sees themselves in some way superior to those around them or struggling to stand out in a crowd. As this particular point of view crystallizes, you'll be better able to see the external circumstances through it. Like the proverbial rose-colored glasses, the character's view will shade the world based on their attitude toward it or their ideas about it.

It's likely that the character's view of the world is different than your own, maybe drastically so. Whether they are relatable to you personally or not, that character is probably the hero of their own story, or at least its center. To them, this point of view is a perfectly natural response to their world. This can be particularly difficult if those views repulse you. For example, if your character's understanding of home is one of safety, love, food, acceptance and warmth, but your personal experience of home was more transient and filled with fear, uncertainty, and harm—then home is a concept to be reconciled between actor and character. If their views are unaligned with your own, remember that empathy doesn't require you to adopt their point of view wholesale as if it were your own. You don't have to like them in order to more fully understand them.

The events of the play may test and alter that point of view, so it will be useful for you to crystalize that particular point of view at the beginning of the play's story and track any shifts that happen along the way. Often, plays contain moments of revelation or transformation that reorient a character to their circumstances, forcing them to respond completely differently to a world that may not have changed in the eyes of other characters. If a character has suddenly pierced the veil of their old life, they may see systems and forces at work that were previously invisible. How will they respond now that they can no longer unsee the corruption of leaders, the hypocrisy of role models, or the flimsiness of their carefully constructed sense of self?

Exercise 3.4: A Particular Point of View

It's not always easy to identify what circumstances are most relevant to the play before you've explored them. Once you have, these more pressing circumstances may help you clarify the character's point of view. Now that you've generated some ideas about their circumstances, try to determine which are having the strongest influence on the character over the course of the play. Using the information you've gathered so far, sort out what has the biggest impact on your character as they begin the action of the play. Try responding to the prompts, from the character's perspective and in their voice:

- How would you describe your life to someone you wanted to be honest with? How would you describe a typical day?
- What are important places in your typical day? Places that bring you joy? Places that evoke frustration or anger?
- Looking back, what are the most significant factors that led you to this point in your life?
- What circumstances would need to change for you to live a life you'd find more ideal?
- Is there something about your life that you are reminded of every day?
- To what degree do you feel you have control over your circumstances or have the ability to change them? Why? Who has control, if not you?

Let the answers to these prompts guide you in this next set of prompts. Here, we'll try to get a stronger sense of the character's point of view at the beginning of the play's action:

- What do you know to be true about the world? What can you always be certain of?

- Where is the most important place for this character to feel empowered and strong? What place do they feel the weakest?
- What has been life's biggest lesson for you so far? What advice would you give to someone who is living a life like yours?
- What should be changed in this world? Why?
- Where is your place in this world? How do you fit into it?
- Do you notice something that other people tend to overlook?
- What one person would you call in a moment of extreme emotion? What person would you never call under those circumstances?

Now, consider the character at or near the end of the play's action. Ask the same questions from the previous sections. What has changed? What prompted these changes? How does your character feel about these changes? Bear in mind that some of your characters' ideas may not have changed so much as intensified.

As we bring this part of the conversation to a close, it is important to contemplate why we feel comfortable in the places and situations we do. What our place is in our families, our social communities, our culture, and our country are all tied and linked to our given circumstances. What does home mean to each of us? These questions are important for our own self-awareness as well as for understanding the characters we bring to life on stage. Understanding place is intrinsic to our sense of self. The essential nature of place is due in part to the fact that it is one of life's few constants. You can see this deep-seated relationship to nature in "the claim made long ago by phenomenologists that sense of place is a natural condition of human existence (dwelling = being), an invariant in a changing world" (Lewicka 209). How we understand the world and how we create that understanding for our characters is inextricably linked to the way we perceive fitting in (or not) to the places we live and encounter.

Further Reading

Hay, Robert. "Sense of Play in Developmental Context." *Journal of Environmental Psychology*, vol. 18, 1998, pp. 5–29.

Lewicka, Maria. "Place Attachment: How Far Have We Come in the Last 40 Years?" *Journal of Environmental Psychology*, vol. 31, no. 3, 2011, pp. 207–230.

Low, Setha M. and Irwin Altman. "Place Attachment: A Conceptual Inquiry." *Place Attachment*, edited by Irwin Altman and Setha M. Low, New York: Plenum Press, 1992, 1–12.

Tuck, Eve and Marcia McKenzie. *Place in Research: Theory, Methodology, and Methods*. New York: Routledge, 2015.

Quick Definitions

Affect: The experience of feeling.

Context: The circumstances of a story. The place, time, setting, and facts of a character's lived reality.

Dominant culture: The set of norms and expectations established and upheld by dominant groups and demanded of subordinate groups.

Given circumstances: The facts provided by the playwright about the characters and world of the play as well as those supplied from a director or designer. Other circumstances are derived from the actor's research and imagination.

Place: A connection to a physical space or location as well as the people, memories, and social or cultural expectations.

Chapter 4

Gender Theory and Relationships

This chapter moves us away from normative binary language when talking about relationships and identity. Allowing our characters to access and embrace a full spectrum of personal identities and relationships provides more depth, potential understanding, and representation to our characters and their worlds.

On a still chilly spring morning, my best friend and I are walking down a street filled with sounds, sights, and smells. Some of these impressions take my notice, most drift past as we talk. We come to the corner and just as we get there, the sign lights up, "Don't Walk." The flash of a smile from my friend lets me know they are going to ignore the sign.

The world around us is in a constant state of flux, filling our senses with steady streams of new information and impressions. The smell of rain in the air, the sudden sound of a car engine turning over, or the sight of mischievous smile. These pieces of sensory input filter through the tint of our unique *point of view* and rebound within us, provoking internal and external reactions. Knowing a character is, in part, knowing how they respond to these external stimuli and the internal changes the stimuli provoke.

The previous chapters have helped us understand how social location and place attachment can impact a character's reaction to stimuli differently than we might. When I smell oncoming rain as I walk down the sidewalk, I may be reminded of watching storms on the porch with my grandfather. The rush of memory makes me want to breathe deep, shorten my steps, and look up. My character, however, is reminded of the discomfort of sitting through class with sodden clothes from a long walk to school, which makes them want to curse under their breath, speed up their pace, and look down at the sidewalk.

Exploring *relationships* allows us to dive deep into one of the most vital sets of given circumstances in a character's life. Knowing *who I am* in relation to *who I am with* shapes my behavior with the other person. It affects the internal responses I have to the things they do and the external actions I perform in response to them. That is to say, when the "Don't Walk" sign suddenly lights up and my friend flashes me that smile, *who I am in relation to that friend* and *who they are to me* matter a great deal in how I feel and what comes next.

In that example, if our relationship hinges on my being a cautious counterbalance to my friend's recklessness, then when I see that smile, I might feel sudden dread and an urge to grab their arm before they run into traffic. If we've lived a lifetime of dares and double dares, I might feel a sudden exhilaration at that smile, pushing my friend back as I try to get a head start into the traffic. In either event, our *relationship* sets up my feelings and the corresponding action I take.

Because of their influence on both a character's particular point of view and their relationships, this chapter will also include an exploration of *gender*, *sex*, and *attraction*. This chapter provides a way to analyze a character's identity as it relates to their gender, sex, and attraction and the implications of those identities on their relationships as they play out in script or performance. This chapter will also deepen concepts established earlier to further mold a character's unique standpoint while also considering how (or whether) that unique social location is expressed in the moment by moment shifts in identity and relationships.

The way I walk down that same street shifts if I am a romantic partner rather than a friend. It changes further still if I am a sibling, a child, an employer. Yes, I can be all these things at once, but some aspect of my identity may also predominate based on circumstances ranging from *who I am with* to *what I am wearing* to *how I feel today*. We all have a multitude of subtle nuances to our identities and relationships that can surface in a given moment for whatever reason, and so will our characters.

Gender, Sex, and Attraction and Character Analysis

It's easy to assume that everyone shares a universal view of gender, sex, and attraction that is like our own, but this is far from true. As this chapter will elaborate, gender is a social construction specific to a time and place which does not neatly map on top of biological sex. Attraction and gender expression are also independent of gender and biological sex, and gender expression is responsive to social context. All of this means that you should not assume your character's experience of gender, sex, and attraction is anything like your own any more than you should assume that of your classmates. As with previous chapters, these traits are particular to them and their circumstances.

In *Gender Trouble: Feminism and the Subversion of Identity,* queer theorist, Judith Butler calls out the normative, hegemonic body as having been created through a "set of repeated acts within a highly rigid regulatory frame that congeal over time to produce the appearance of substance, of a natural sort of being" (45). Butler's warning of repetition of a constructed "natural" should be a warning to us as artists. Our unquestioned presumption of a cis, heterosexuality that adheres to traditional ideals of the masculine/feminine binary leaves our characters to replicate and reproduce heteronormative identities and relationships. While the language may not have been present in earlier generations or in the canon of plays, it doesn't mean the characters didn't consciously or subconsciously experience a spectrum of gender expression, identity and attraction.

The following exercise invites you to begin an orientation with these concepts by allowing you to make a self-inventory. There are several visual resources that explore gender identity (Sam Killerman's "The Genderbread Person" v.4 and Trans Student Educational Resources "The Gender Unicorn"). Both resources are open-access and are routinely updated to map changes in language and understanding as well as provide a helpful way to visualize the interrelated but not interdependent aspects of gender and attraction.

Exercise 4.1: Understanding Your Gender, Sex, and Attraction

For this exercise, make a preliminary inventory of the way you experience Gender Identity, Gender Expression, Anatomical Sex, and Attraction. Assign each slider below a value of 0 to 10 and give yourself a number for each slider that suits you best based on your current understanding of each term. Remember that this is just a preliminary inventory. You may be confused or uncertain about definitions or what values to assign them, even to yourself. That's fine. Simply revise after you've read the material. Also, understand that this inventory is not static. Our identity, expression, and attraction can shift from day-to-day or year-to-year.

As with the previous chapters, understanding your own positionality with regard to gender, sex, and attraction is important to character analysis. Our own preferences may reveal biases or assumptions and choices that we may assume for our characters or not even consider. As with standpoint and place theories, we must be aware of how our own identity impacts and frames the choices we offer our characters.

Exercise 4.1 is a simple way to do a personal assessment and it is a great exercise for characters as well. All too often, if the text does not explicitly state otherwise, theatre artists will

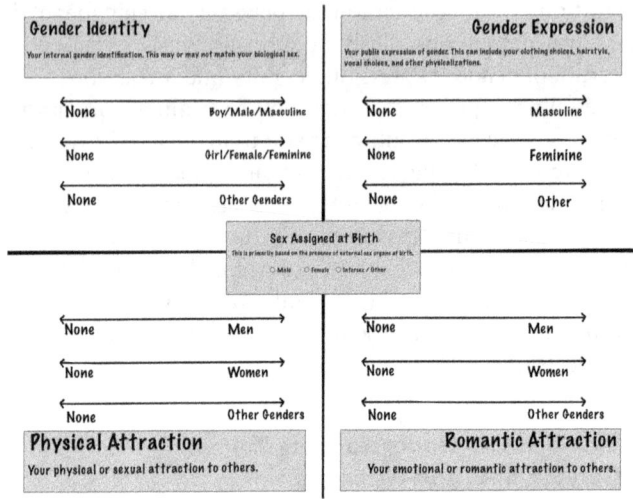

Figure 4.1 Identity, Expression, Attraction Preliminary Inventory

assume a default straight, cis character, who expresses gender in the traditional modes of the actor's own social context. This can be challenged in your character analysis by asking the questions below without assuming you know the answer. Remember you may have begun this work in exercise 3.2.

- How does my character's society view gender, and what are society's expectations of them based on this?
- How does my character experience gender, and how does that relate to their assigned at birth sex?
- How does my character's society view sexuality, and what does that mean for my character's sexual or romantic attractions?
- What are the relevant expectations of gender expression for my character, and does my character deviate from them?
- How closely does my character's view or experience match the dominant ideology of their social context?

As in the previous sections, finding answers to these questions will be a matter of closely reading the text with attention to gender, sex, and attraction. This time the play's setting and time period may provoke you to research in order to learn about expectations of gender and attraction that the character would take for granted or sexual mores that may be ingrained in the character's mind. All this helps you sharpen your character's particular point of view, allowing you to see how they view others and themselves, and it helps you determine whether your character is reconciled to the status quo around them.

If you find that they are in a privileged position in their social context, you could ask how that privilege plays out in their lives. If they are more marginalized, to what degree does that cause them pain and to what degree (if at all) are they able to find a benefit in their social position? Is there a place where they find community? Are there other contexts where they feel more at ease? When you have a sense of the answers to these questions, you're better able to see how your character relates to other characters in the world of the play.

You should not assume a contemporary play contains identical constructions of gender and attraction that match your own. This attention to social constructions then allows you to not only interrogate your own assumptions, but begin the imaginative perspective-taking required to see assumptions and constructs of someone else.

With the coming exercises, you'll begin to map what femaleness and maleness are for both yourself and the character, discerning to what degree both you and your character identifies femaleness and maleness. This process should challenge you to think beyond a binary choice between a universal femaleness and a universal maleness as you determine this critical component of your character's identity.

This chapter also asks you to explore gender as a performative (which is not to say untruthful) expression of gender identity. As gender activist and performance artist, Kate Bornstein says,

> We need to do away with any system of gender that pressures us into believing that we are imperfectly gendered. The gender I'm perfectly happy with keeping around is the gender I live with that shifts on its own accord as I move forward in time and space. After all, our genders are one of many ways that we interface with others, and with our surroundings. I believe that if we simply trust ourselves to shift, sure enough, our genders will shift as we need them to. (xviii)

Bornstein points out the fluidity of gender as connected to social groups, place, and relationships. Allowing our characters the same sense of fluidity is imperative to a fully realized character. We need to consider how we enact a kind of fluid and ever-changeable role playing of both what you and your characters would consider feminine and masculine behaviors. In this way, you can begin to map out the ways in which your character performs their own spectrum of feminine and masculine behaviors in a nuanced flux as they try to achieve some goal. As we will see, this is not too unlike, and certainly related to, the beat by beat actions a character takes in the service of their objectives (concepts which we will be handling in Chapters 5 and 6). Here, however, the objective will most often be to express to or conceal from others their identity for some purpose.

Clarifying Language

Establishing first that gender is a social construction specific to a time, place, and cultural context, we must first explore what gender means for ourselves, then compare whether gender means the same thing for our characters. Instead of offering a binary look at these distinctions, this chapter asks you to think in terms of spectrum-oriented identities (refer back to Figure 4.1), which allow for the possibility of "and" rather than binary alignment that focuses on "or" relationships. For example, my gender presentation may be more femme *and* I may be emotionally attracted to men *and* physically attracted to both masculine *and* feminine individuals.

In *Undoing Gender*, Judith Butler explains, "Language has a dual possibility: it can be used to assert a true and inclusive universality of persons, or it can institute a hierarchy in which only some persons are eligible to speak and others, by virtue of their exclusion from the universal point of view, cannot 'speak' without simultaneously deauthorizing that speech" (164). How we begin to use non-binary, non-normative language to talk about gender, sex, and attraction creates space for our characters (whether historical or contemporary) to express themselves and their relationships. The playwright may rely upon hierarchical language of exclusion (binary/or language rather than spectrum/and language), but that doesn't mean the character's interior monolog and/or subtext can't move to a more inclusive viewpoint regarding gender, sex, and attraction. As with our relationship conversation, these identity markers are fluid and can shift based on social location, place attachment, groupings, and/or our comfort levels within these situations.

Core Relationship

No one is an island. We are connected to the other people in our lives by invisible threads that help us locate who we are based on how we relate to others. Yes, there is much that you can define about yourself alone—I am a fan of old movies, I am a horticulturist, I am a dog person. To get a fuller picture of who you are, however, you'd have to put other people in the frame. Part of building *who you are* as a person depends on *who you are in **relation** to other people.* If I am a student, who is my teacher? If I am a son, who are my parents? I am ____'s sister, I am ____'s friend, I am ____'s employee, I am ____'s lover. The same is true for characters on stage.

92 Gender Theory and Relationships

At first, defining your character's relationships to the other characters in the play is simple because we tend to have simple overarching relationships with other people that stay relatively fixed. Tamara and Sheryl are sisters. Amir and Mabel are friends. Dev is Carmen's employee. It would take a significant event to change these relationships. As it is so central to the way a person defines their relationship to another, it is helpful to think of this fixed overarching relationship as the *core relationship*.

Exercise 4.2: Mapping Relationship Constellations, Part One

Start a relationship map by placing your name in a small circle at the center of a blank piece of paper. Around your name circle, place the names of several people from different

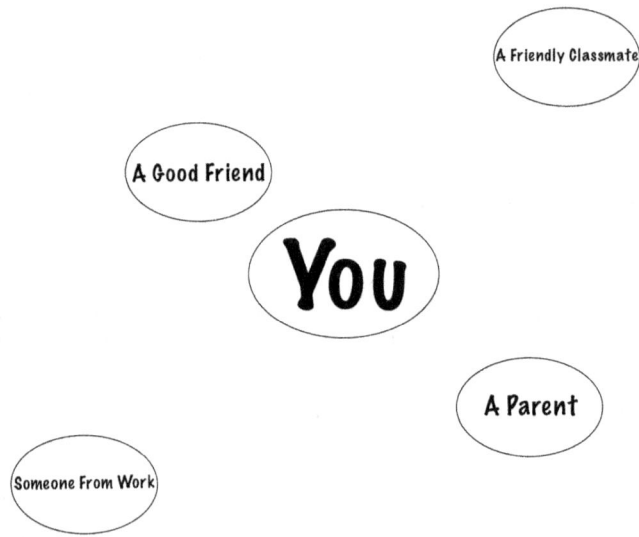

Figure 4.2 Relationship Map 1

parts of your life in circles of their own. This doesn't need to be a comprehensive representation of all the people in your life. In fact, it's better to take one or two people from different areas of your life (family, friends, class, work, social organizations) in order to represent a broad variety of relationships. Place these names at varying distances from the center as a representation of how close you feel to this person.

Here's what a start might look like:

Now, connect these names with lines. Above the line, label the relationship by putting down who that person is to you. Try pushing beyond the simple title of this relationship in order to add nuance and flavor to the relationship to make it more specific. This could connect you by physical or romantic attraction, similarities in gender expression, or any other connection. Below the line, label the relationship by who you believe you are to them. For now, simply notice those relationships and whether or not those relationships correspond to the distance between your circle and theirs. Here are a few examples:

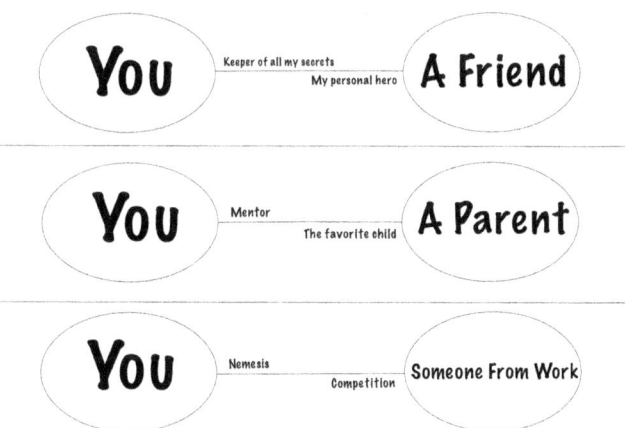

Figure 4.3 Relationship Map 2

Seismic Shifts, Changes in Core Relationships

The core relationship sets the tone and parameters for our interactions with another person. We behave differently with our friends than we do with our parents even if we have deep love for both. Because our core relationships are so central to our interactions with others, those relationships persist in different contexts and most events. A strong bond of friendship weathers a fight, and so Amir and Mabel can argue a great deal and maintain that core relationship. They are playfully sarcastic with each other, they laugh without disdain, and because of their shared history, they can mock each other without damage. They fight as friends. Carmen and Dev meet up outside of work for a party, but have a difficult time forgetting their boss-employee dynamic. Carmen feels she must maintain an air of professionalism and Dev is excessively deferential. They can't quite let loose in front of each other even in a party atmosphere.

Of course, even a deeply ingrained relationship is vulnerable to significant changes, events in life of such magnitude may alter the conditions of the core relationship and transform it into something else. Amir and Mabel have a falling out over an irreconcilable difference of opinions that came up in one of their usually friendly arguments. They have difficulty forgiving each other for what feels like a deep betrayal and an antagonism grows between them. Slowly, the friends become enemies. Dev's work has been stellar and revealed talents that Carmen did not initially recognize. Seeing that they share an interest in design, she wants to leave her stifling career and go into business with him as a creative partner. All of a sudden, they go to work as equals.

Over time or in a flash, the terms of a core relationship can change. As a result, the behaviors and interactions must change, too. Now enemies, Amir and Mabel no longer pull punches when they argue. Their sarcasm is venomously superior, they mock each other outright, and because of their previous relationship, they both know just what to do to get under one another's skin. They fight with the gloves off. Carmen and Dev make plans to meet up outside of work now because they feel more at ease without the boss-employee dynamic hanging over them. They share ideas with alacrity and the joy of mutual respect.

Like a palimpsest, on which text has been erased to make room for something new but the impression of the old text remains, traces of the previous core relationship still exist within the newly reconfigured relationship. These traces further shade the dynamics between people. Going back to Tamara and Sheryl, for example, the sisters behave as sisters throughout most of their young lives. Abruptly, they lose their mother and the depth of that loss requires them, consciously or not, to reconstruct their *core relationship*. Tamara, the older of the two, begins to act as a mother to Sheryl. Nevertheless, they have a history as sisters that persists in the newly formed mother-daughter relationship. This *(sisters) mother-daughter* relationship causes Tamara to resent the need to parent her own sister or causes Sheryl to challenge Tamara's authority when tensions run high. Sheryl's behaviors may vacillate between playing up the childishness her sister projects onto her and trying to reclaim adulthood from Tamara. Tamara's behaviors skew toward instructional, proscriptive, and even commanding. A change in the relationship changes the actions of those in it.

Plays often dramatize these shifting dynamics in relationships. You can find vibrant examples of this in the dynamic between Nick and Bashir in Ayad Akhtar's *The Invisible Hand*, Cynthia and Tracey in Lynn Nottage's *Sweat*, or within the family of Taylor Mac's *Hir*. In your own analysis, it is vital for you to find the core relationship and track any changes to that essential dynamic. Bear in mind, these shifts may occur off stage or before the action of the play. Once you know where they are, it will be easier for you to consider the effect that these shifts have on your character.

Exercise 4.3: Mapping Relationship Constellations, Part Two

Repeat Exercise 4.2, but this time with your character in the center and every other character arrayed around them. Remember to consider distance and to be specific with the over-line and under-line descriptions. The details can excite the imagination and add specificity to your analysis.

Now, track the changes in these relationships, if any. Where in the script do you find these shifts? What prompts them? Pinpoint as best as you can the moment of the dynamic shift between the characters. What is the new over-line and under-line relationship dynamic? Again, these changes may have happened off stage or even before the events of the play itself.

Core Relationship and Actions

When building or analyzing a character, the core relationship is a very specific lens through which one character views another character in the world of the play. For an actor, it is a primary factor in determining the tactics you have available to you as the character when you are in pursuit of an objective and another character stands in your way. It also colors the way that your character *reacts* to the actions and words of another character.

If we imagine Amir and Mabel to be friends again (through a miracle of forgiveness and mutual respect) and that Mabel is withholding some juicy secret that Amir wants desperately to know, his tactics for getting the secret from her are limited within the conditions of their core relationship. You might think of it as drawing a circle around "friends." Actions beyond that circle's edge are unlikely, but not impossible. If Amir were to do something outside of that circle, it would at the very least shock Mabel. It may even change the nature of their core relationship.

Simply put, certain actions fit within that circle, others fall outside. Amir might beg for the secret, he might try to coax it from her, but it is less likely that he flirts with Mabel in an effort to seduce the information out of her. Seduction lies beyond the edge of their circle. It might force them to re-evaluate the parameters of their relationship. The heightened and emotionally charged circumstances of a play regularly push characters from tactics within the circle to actions that lie beyond it. In that event, the characters have created a dramatic shift in their relationship and a new dynamic is created. Knowing what is within the circle and what is beyond it is a way of detecting significant shifts in relationship dynamics and a way of performing those shifts.

Exercise 4.4: In the Circle and Out of the Circle

Take a moment to identify one relationship in your character's life and a shared scene from your play. If this exercise is part of a scene study, use your scene. In Chapters 5 and 6, we'll go into more detail about objectives and actions, but for now, simply identify what you think your character wants from the other character in this scene. Try expressing it as the title on a sheet of paper. Below the title, put the names of the characters and their relationship.

Draw a circle about half the size of the sheet. Now, brainstorm a variety of ways your character could get what they want from the other character. For now, write without regard to whether you think they would or would not carry out any given action; you might be surprised at how your sense of what a character would do can change. Fill the circle with possible actions that suit the relationship for these two characters. Write actions that are inappropriate (but still possible) outside the circle.

Going forward, note any time you feel your character is compelled to operate outside of the circle. What triggers this shift or change? What does this do to the relationship? Is it significant enough to change the relationship dynamic? What feelings might it provoke between characters?

Role Playing and Gender Expression

If the *core relationship* is more stable over time, *role playing* allows for a far more fluid relationship dynamic. Role playing is a kind of action itself that alters the relationship dynamic temporarily and (usually) without lasting consequences for the conditions of the core relationship. It can be consciously performative or unconsciously assumed in an instant only to be dropped again moments later. Generally, it is associated, as are other actions, with the character trying to get something that they want.

While core relationships are built up over time, role playing tends to serve an immediate need. As a result, the action of role playing is determined by context, the immediacy of given circumstances like where and when a character is right now. On their first day working as peers in Carmen's home office, she plays at being a *tour guide* to show Dev around while also putting him at ease in their new context. Later, they go out for drinks and Dev plays a *reporter* in order to get Carmen to open up about her life. At the end of the night, Dev has had too much to drink and Carmen plays at *parenting* him when he reaches for his keys in order to protect him.

As all actions can, role playing can also alter the conditions of the core relationship, but primarily, it is a way of injecting fluidity to that relationship without necessarily aiming to alter it. Identifying when a character is role playing can help you more acutely identify the actions they may play as a result. Sometimes, a character can play at being an antagonist for another character as a way of pushing their friend or egging them on, but this doesn't mean they've abandoned their role as an ally to their friend. They've simply made an adjustment to the usual roles in order to meet some need that they've identified, motivating their friend.

Though not perfectly analogous, role playing maps most closely with *gender expression*, how a person expresses their gender through physical appearance (clothing, hair, make-up, behavior), and are often adjusted based on context or a specific need. Characters can assume more femininity, masculinity, or neutrality in the performance of certain actions as a way of expressing their identity, masking it, or for the purpose of achieving some goal.

The characteristics traditionally associated with femininity or masculinity do not reside within a person based on biological sex. They are cultural constructs and can be assumed by anyone. Therefore, characters can adopt actions, attitudes, and other outward signifiers of femininity, masculinity, or neutrality regardless of how they identify. Furthermore, characters may express a blend that doesn't neatly fit into this binary.

Exercise 4.5: Gender Expectations

The next two exercises work together or separately, but the first provides a richer foundation for the second. For the first exercise, you are examining gender under your own cultural context. To begin, spread out a long sheet of blank paper. If you do this as a group exercise (and you should), you'll need a lot of paper. Draw a horizontal line down the middle with room above and below. Assign one end as "hyperfeminine" and the other end as "hyper-masculine." Consider the space toward the middle and above the line as a place of blending

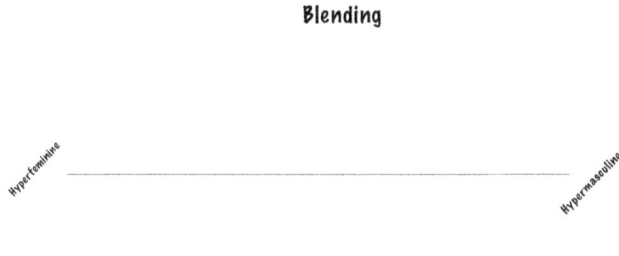

Figure 4.4 Gender Expectations Map

(of masculinity and femininity) and below the line as less specifically gendered or non-gendered.

Remember we are charting these items in relation to society's expectations of gender and gender expression. If you find yourself repeatedly categorizing items as a non-gendered, challenge yourself to truly examine whether or not society as a whole really does exclude this item from gender. Ask yourself "How would someone who holds traditional definitions of femininity and masculinity would label this?" If that still leads you to answer non-gendered, that is still useful information.

Now, take any category (examples in a moment) and try to map several items from each category and identify its position on your map according to social and cultural expectations. If you are working with others, let disagreements fuel discussion while you try to agree on specific coordinates. And remember, you might decide that the coordinate should rightly hover an inch above the page.

Categories to try—clothing, shapes, animals, foods, textures, smells, words, actions, occupations, and well-known people.

To get your started:

- Clothing: tank top, jeans, high tops, suit jacket, boots
- Actions: punch, tug, dance, leap, trip
- Occupations: teacher, doctor, garbage collector, lawyer, soldier, athlete

Are there things that you were surprised carried gendered expectations? Why do you think an idea falls toward an extreme? Do you think certain categories would map out differently 20 years ago? 50? More?

Exercise 4.6: My Character's Gender Expressions and Role Playing

Now, explore your character in the context of a scene. If you have not already done so, you'll need to consider a few important questions for this exercise, namely:

What are the gender expectations for your character in their particular social and cultural context?

How do they experience gender, sex, and attraction themselves? How do they experience gender, sex, and attraction in the company of others?

How well does your character fit in with the expectations of their social and cultural context?

Identify what your character wants in this scene, paying special attention to any shifts that this may take in the middle of the scene. For the purposes of this exercise, imagine that the character is always playing some role (review earlier definition and example of role playing), and track the changes of that role in this scene. Note what the character thinks they can get from playing the role and what forces them to reevaluate their role playing.

Next, note where in the gender spectrum (previously established in Exercise 4.5) your character is expressing at any given point. Again, note what your character thinks they can get from this and what prompts a change. Do any shifts in role playing coincide with shifts in gender expression? What does that tell you about the character or the scene?

Building the Specifics of the Core Relationship

Often we leave a relationship broadly defined and inadvertently assume a universal understanding of that relationship as if, for example, a father-son relationship means the same thing to the character as it does for you. In fact, our relationships are inevitably more complex than a simple label can express. Adding depth to your performance or your analysis will require you to determine the subtle shadings and nuances that abound in the space between characters. There is no set tone for any given relationship, not all parent-child dynamics are based on love and affection any more than all antagonistic relationships are based on violent hatred. So, determining a specific dynamic for a particular relationship is key to playing the interactions between characters. Start with a mind toward broad generalizations and gradually build up the finer details.

In part, we can discover the nuances of a relationship and the resulting dynamic by asking what each person wants or receives from the other. If Dev only wants a paycheck from Carmen, his behavior is bound to be different than it would be if he wants Carmen to validate his creative ideas. If Sheryl wants Tamara to be proud of her, her behaviors may be subtly different even from a version of Sheryl that wants Tamara to respect her. As you analyze a character's relationship, ask what they get from that relationship and whether they are getting what they want from it. Specifically, ask from the character's point of view:

What do I want from this relationship?

What do I actually get from this relationship?

How different is *what I get* from *what I want*?

We can imagine a wide variety of different friendships for Amir and Mabel in order to give their dynamic more clarity. In so doing, we can determine the actions that fit within that dynamic. Perhaps their friendship is based on a desire for competition, so they are *competitive friends*. The two walk down the street subtly jockeying for leadership as they look for a place to eat. Mabel tests Amir at any opportunity and so when she asks him questions she does so with a tone that suggests she knows something he doesn't. Amir flaunts any small advantage and so when he answers, he does so in a way that is intended to pop Mabel's ego.

Adding even more detail, we could consider whether their friendship might be a relatively balanced competition in which they bring out the best in one another through minor challenges. Otherwise, it may be a lopsided competition in which Amir feels the need to prove himself to Mabel who, in turn, might enjoy the feeling of superiority. In either case, they are *competitive friends* but exploring how well-balanced that competition is reveals a great deal about who they are to one another and what each wants from the other.

Alternatively, the friendship between Mabel and Amir could be based on affection, respect, envy, symbiosis, or a wide range of other dynamics, each with their own particular shading. It's also important to note here that Amir and Mabel do not necessarily view the friendship the same way or get the same thing from its dynamic. For one thing, one of them may see this relationship as a burgeoning romance, while the other does not. We don't always agree about the tone and type of the relationship we are in.

For another thing, their dynamic might give each of them something else. Amir may see himself as mentoring Mabel, getting satisfaction from helping her navigate life. So, Amir may see Mabel as *Friend and Protégé*. Contrastingly, Mabel may see herself as leader and Amir as her loyal follower, someone she can rely upon to do her tasks. She may see him as *Friend and Sidekick*. In many relationships, there is a dynamic that lends itself to one person taking a more dominant position, while another (by choice or not) takes a subservient position. This is not necessarily a static positioning or a conscious one. Some characters prefer to take the lead in certain moments and relinquish control in others. Some cannot or refuse to make such a change. As noted earlier, these preferences and tendencies are based on many elements including social groups, situated place, and/or positions of power.

Exploring all these details in a relationship begins to reflect back on your character, deepening your understanding of them. If you find your character likes to take the lead a lot, that tells you about who they are, how they think of themselves, and how they feel comfortable behaving in the world. It also gives you a clue to how they feel if they are suddenly pushed out of the role they are accustomed to playing.

Exercise 4.7: Lines of Attraction and Repulsion

Our relationships are difficult to encapsulate with labels, but it is a good place to begin since understanding a character's relationships is vital to understanding who they are and how they behave in the world. Try drawing a circle at one end of a sheet of paper writing a character's name (your character's name) in the center of it. Then, add a similar circle at the other end of the paper with the name of a character who is significant to them.

Again, if this work is part of a specific scene study, use that scene. If you are studying the play more broadly, especially as a director or a designer, then this exercise may be the first step in creating a web of attraction and repulsion as you map out multiple characters.

Finally, draw a faint line between the two. Try to label the relationship between the two of them. Get as specific as you can, but also challenge yourself to make a concise and clear label over the line (your character's view of the other person) and under the line (their view of your character). Now, consider what the dynamic energy between these characters is. Is your character drawn in through this relationship, are they repulsed by it, or are they fairly neutral? Deepen that faint line by turning it into a series of arrows that reflect the energy you see between your character and the other. Here are some examples of how that energy might flow:

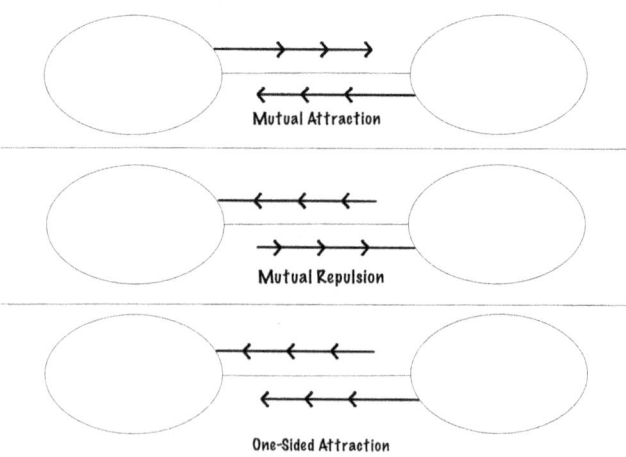

Figure 4.5 Attraction and Repulsion Map 1

This exercise is greatly aided with colors indicating different energies; you might try warm colors for attraction, cool for repulsion, and neutral for neutral. Remember that over the line is not necessarily the same as under.

To broaden out the map, try drawing your character in the center of a large sheet of paper and then add a circle for every other significant character in your character's life. For example:

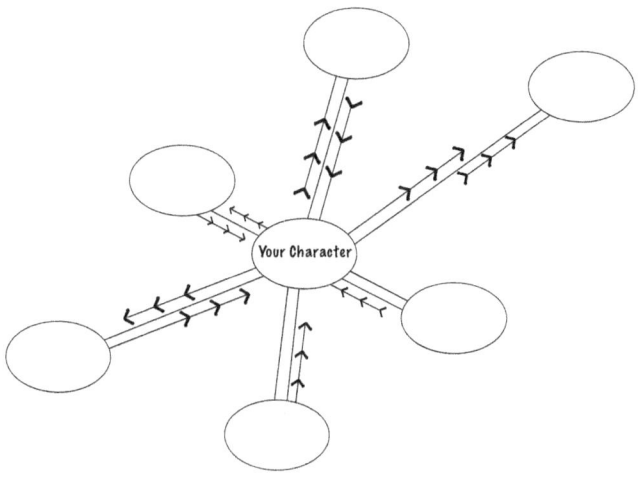

Figure 4.6 Attraction and Repulsion Map 2

Consider the distance between circles here; which relationships are closer and which are more distant? This large series of circles may include characters who never show up in the play, but are often referred to in the text.

As you repeat the exercise for each relationship, what do you notice? Are there distant relationships that your character is trying to pull closer or close relationships that are drifting apart? Does your character have many close relationships, or do you find them relatively isolated in the center? Where do you see the exceptions? How do the pushes and pulls relate to what your character wants from their relationships?

All of this maps out an overarching positioning of one character to another and reveals the dynamic energy between them. Now, you can consider in which ways a character pulls another in or pushes them away. None of this is necessarily known to the characters themselves in such clear terms, but as an actor or simply for your script analysis, it is necessary for you to see more clearly what they may only be aware of subconsciously.

Gender, Sex, Attraction and Character

In the world of any given play, a character is entangled in a web of relationships. Each thread connects them to another character in some established (though changeable) relationship. Those characters may view that relationship very differently, but these connections cannot truly be severed. Even as partnerships end or friends become enemies, these threads of relation only change.

Along every thread flows some dynamic energy, which is usually charged by some force of attraction or repulsion. This attraction or repulsion does not always come from sexual desire or romantic interest, although such charged threads are common in dramatic literature. Characters constantly pull one another closer or push each other away with their actions.

Exploring a character's gender, sex, and attraction is necessary to understanding characters because it helps you situate them in their own web of relationships, are vital components of a character's identity, and have enormous importance on how they engage with the world around them. As we said before, even a very contemporary play may not share your assumptions about gender, sex, or attraction. So, understanding the character's world as they do will require you to consider these aspects of identity very specifically.

Further Reading

Bornstein, Kate. *Gender Outlaw: On Men, Women, and the Rest of Us*. New York: Vintage Books, 2016.

Butler, Judith. *Gender Trouble: Feminism and the Subversion of Identity*. New York: Routledge, 2006.

Butler, Judith. *Undoing Gender*. New York: Routledge, 2004.
GenderSpectrum.org
"Gender Unicorn." *Trans Student Education Resources*, 20 Sept. 2020, www.transstudent.org/gender/.
Killerman, Sam. *The Social Justice Advocate's Handbook: A Guide to Gender*. Austin: Impetus Books, 2017.
Marinucci, Mimi. *Feminism Is Queer: The Intimate Connection between Queer and Feminist Theory*. London: Zed Books, 2016.
Pilcher, Jane and Imelda Whelehan. *Fifty Key Concepts in Gender Studies*. London: Sage Publications, 2016.

Quick Definitions

Binary: Two parts or options

Cisgender: Gender identity matches the sex assigned at birth

Core relationship: Fixed, overarching relationship

Gender: Spectrum of performed identity behaviors and expressions as read by society; we are not born with gender, but learn to perform this social construct

Hegemonic: Dominant

Heteronormative: The assumption that heterosexuality is the default sexual orientation

Role playing: The temporary change to a relationship dynamic where one or both characters assume different roles

Sex: Designation placed on an infant at birth based on visible sex organs; biological and anatomical

Social construction: A collective understanding of an idea or object is widely held by society without question

Spectrum: A scale between two scales or positions

Chapter 5

Class Privilege and Desire

This chapter explores how class privilege impacts a character's objectives. Our wants and needs are largely framed by our economic and class position. Class privilege is often rendered invisible, but a lack of privilege can limit choices and impact nearly every facet of one's life.

Here's the beginning of a very short story:

Miles loves to dance, but he's embarrassed to move in front of people. He spends his week going to classes, hanging out with friends, working a quiet campus job. Some part of him is always waiting for Thursday evening because he has discovered by chance that a remote studio space is left open and no one is ever using it. There, he can turn up music and dance without fear of anyone seeing him.

Until one day someone does. Quite by accident, Aaron passes by the studio, his curiosity takes him inside and he sees Miles dance. When Miles sees this stranger in the doorway, he panics and tries to leave, but Aaron manages to stop him long enough to introduce himself and compliment Miles on his dancing. Aaron recommends classes or meeting with some other dancers that he knows, but Miles explains his reluctance to dance in front of people. Even as he does, he realizes that the same part of him that always looks forward to Thursdays also wants to take Aaron up on his suggestion. So, he agrees to meet up with Aaron next Thursday and get comfortable dancing with just one other person for a start.

And Miles' journey goes from there, following a newly awakened desire to gain comfort dancing in front of others. From this beginning, we can imagine a story unfolding as described in Chapter 1—action growing from this first event, the inciting incident, as Miles pursues a new goal.

At the surface, we have identified that Miles' challenge is to be more confident dancing in public. What factors of class privilege could be linked to Miles' hesitation of dancing in public? If you didn't pause to even think about class in the above scenario, don't be embarrassed. Gregory Mantsios, poverty and inequality scholar, argues, "People in the United States don't like to talk about class. Or so it would seem. We don't speak about class privileges, or class oppression, or the class nature of society. These terms are not part of our everyday vocabulary" (182). If you didn't consider the implications of class and privilege in the above situation, you aren't alone. While Miles may couch his Thursday night solo dance evenings as an embarrassment to dance in public, that embarrassment may reveal economic or class factors at work.

What assumptions did you make about Miles, Aaron, and their economic status? Did you consider whether one was taking out student loans or if one student was a full pay? Did you note that Miles worked a campus job? Did you assume that Miles and Aaron both took dance classes prior to their college experience? If so, what are the implications of those assumptions? Is it easier for Miles to indicate an embarrassment to dance in front of others rather than explain that he isn't formally trained? Or that he can't afford to take a dance class? Or pay for a cover charge to dance with Aaron's friends at a club? As Mantsios indicates above, admitting personal embarrassment is easier and more socially acceptable than explaining any of these economic or class privilege factors.

Prior to the events of a play, the characters likely lived out their lives in some sort of equilibrium. This probably wasn't an inactive state as such, but most likely the characters had a pattern or predictable trajectory to their daily lives that was in some ways stable, as with Miles' pattern of class, work, and friends as he waits for Thursdays. Other characters might spend every day running between two jobs trying to make ends meet and come home at odd hours to unwind and others yet may have family money that allows them to focus only on their education while simultaneously spoiling themselves with luxuries, always searching for a new thrill. Like Miles, the characters may well have desires that pull on them to break this established pattern, but before the events that set off this play, they probably haven't developed the motivation or found the access (economically or otherwise) to pursue those desires, or else they haven't found a way to realize them.

A pattern of behavior, then, creates a relatively balanced state in the lives of the characters, one which the conflict of the play will throw off. Even if the characters' circumstances meant that life was quite chaotic around them, prior to the events of this play that chaos was contained in some sort of overall balance. This means they could reasonably expect to live life as they had been living it lately before the events of the play. The soldiers and civilians of Rajiv Joseph's *Bengal Tiger at the Baghdad Zoo*, for example, have lived quite chaotic lives in the months since the U.S. invasion of Iraq. Nevertheless, they have found a pattern prior to the events of the play that keeps their lives on a certain trajectory that is somewhat stable. Even though everything is perched on a precipice and poised to fall disastrously, it hasn't tipped yet. Many plays begin poised in this way, ready to tip and fall into something new.

Then, something happens near the beginning of the play, or even just before, which upsets that relative balance. That *inciting incident,* the moment that sets the play's conflict into motion, changes the character's life in some fundamental way. This event could take many forms. A new opportunity arises, allowing the character to realize some deep desire. A need is awakened within a character, growing and demanding to be fulfilled. Perhaps the character has lost something and seeks to restore it. Whatever the case may be, the pattern of their old life is broken. Now, they are set on a new trajectory which demands new actions from them.

A character's needs, wants, aims, and desires propel them through the action of the play. For some characters eating may be a relatively small and mundane task, as in a desire to eat. For others, eating may be a high order need for the day as they didn't eat the day before due to limited access to funds and/or food. Failing to note the differences in "eating" as a need for our characters presumes a generic, but acceptable, middle class. Mantsios argues that the middle class is an acceptable social group because "they mute class difference" (150). A social agreement on a generic middle class that we can speak about and discuss provides us a way of "gloss[ing] over differences" (Mantsios 150). This broadly written middle class also avoids "any suggestion of conflict or injustice" (150) and allows the middle-class trope to maintain its seemingly "neutral" and invisible power.

Just as Chapter 4 has allowed space to consider the influence of gender, sex, and attraction on a character's life, this chapter will look at the relationship of class privilege and a character's desires. As before, this does not mean that we've selected class for this chapter because it is the only or even the strongest aspect of identity that influences a character's desires. It is simply another aspect of a character's identity, existing inextricably together with the others. As such, you should remember that facets of identity like gender are still present here, as class will still affect both Chapters 4 and 6.

Desire

The central component for this chapter is desire. We'll examine a character's needs and wants in order to better understand how desires provoke a character to action. For that reason, this chapter will be closely intertwined with Chapter 6, which focuses on action. Stanislavski illustrated this interconnectedness of desire and action when he described *tasks*. At several points, he stresses that a task, more commonly translated and understood as an *objective*, arises out of a character's need to overcome an obstacle to their desire, and therefore, must be *active* (143–149). Simply put, your character may want to be happy, but "to be" is passive and doesn't address a specific obstacle to that happiness. A passive construction simply doesn't give the character sufficient agency and drive because there's no inherent activity. It also lacks direction and specificity; it doesn't suggest anything a character will do to attain that happiness or address any obstacles to that happiness.

Alternatively, a more active task than "to be happy" might be something like "to pursue" or "to find" happiness. These verbs suggest something more active that the character is going to do in order to get what they want. What's more, you can direct these actions against an obstacle which currently prevents that character's happiness. If, for example, the given circumstances suggest that your character is isolated, then a task might be *to pursue happiness by making friends*, or it could be *to find happiness by finding a way to enjoy my solitude*.

Adding to this example, investigating whether the character is feeling isolated due to class privilege is also important. Does the character feel isolated due to working two jobs in order to pay for basic living expenses and thus doesn't have time to socialize? The task might shift slightly *to pursue happiness by making friends or social connections at work* or it could be *to find happiness by relishing the time in my home that I alone have provided.* Not every desire has an economic or privilege factor, but pushing to explore potential class factors could provide depth and texture to the character and their world.

It's important to note that you are better served by framing tasks in a positive construction. Let's say your character has a secret and they are keeping it to themselves as in this short scenario: *Miles doesn't want Marie to know where he's been on Thursday nights, but she keeps asking him questions about what he's been up to.* You might be inclined to say that Miles' task is *to not tell Marie his secret.* While there's truth to that, it doesn't suggest action. As a construction "to not do" doesn't actually suggest a specific action. If you know Miles doesn't want to give away his secret, a task like *to evade Marie's questions* actually suggests action on Miles' part rather than inaction.

So, in this chapter, we'll look at desire as setting up *tasks* in much the same way that Stanislavski suggests. That means desires will immediately imply actions to fulfill them. We'll look for small tasks and consider how they relate to ever larger tasks. Finally, we'll frame those actions in positive, active constructions and orient them toward obstacles. Throughout all of these steps, we should take the time to consider the potential class and economic privileges or deprivileges present in the world of the play.

To get started, we'll consider the event that kindles the action of the play—the *inciting incident*. For the play as a whole, the inciting incident is an event that sets off the action of the play broadly speaking. It's the meeting of two people who make an intense connection; it is the death that brings the far-flung family back together; it is some new opportunity that sets the central characters on a new path. If your character is the protagonist, one of several protagonists, or otherwise central to the story's action, this inciting event is particularly relevant to you. However, you may also be analyzing a character who is set on their current path long before, or even part way through the play as a reaction to something that happens along the way. The first two exercises of this chapter will help you identify your character's personal inciting incident and what new desire that event sparked.

Exercise 5.1: Inciting Incidents, Part One

Identifying the inciting incident for the play means first identifying what the story is. Is this a play about a personal discovery? A blossoming romance? The tragic dissolution of a family? The destruction of a nation? Or a way of life? Start by identifying what the story's main action is in a clear and simple way. This can be difficult because so much can happen in a play that you may feel the need to account for it all. But, this isn't a summary. Rather, you're trying to distill the action down to its essence.

Try writing "this play is about..." and then add about 7–10 more words. For example,

- This play is about... *a woman struggling to overcome bias in her field.*
- This play is about... *a family mending itself after traumatic loss.*
- This play is about... *the birth of a new era.*

Next, look at the central verb—in the above examples, "struggling," "mending," and "birth." Consider whether this verb is both (a) the most accurate word for the action of the play, and (b) excites your imagination. Play around with other words until you find something that feels right to you. Also check in with a thesaurus if you struggle to name the right action.

Now, consider who does this action. Identifying who struggles to overcome bias may be easy, but if the action of your play involves the efforts of many people, it may not be so clear. If the family is mending itself, you might have to ask whether everyone is working toward that end. If you're looking at a play that is about the birth of a new era, there may be several characters working toward something that can bring that era into being.

Once you have distilled the central action of the play and identified the primary characters in this action, it's time to ask how this all got started. What was the event that set the character or characters on this path? How do you account for their current trajectory? Look for an event near the beginning of the play or even before it that sparked this action. Remember to find the event that started the action of the play, not necessarily the one that created the given circumstances. In the above example of the family mending itself, you might be inclined to say that the tragic loss was the inciting event. That may be true, but it also may be the loss broke the family apart and a separate event actually set the family on the path of mending that break. Try expressing that inciting incident in a simple sentence as well.

If you have that event identified, you should (with a little editing) be able to craft a simple two-part sentence from that inciting incident and the central action you identified earlier. Here are examples from the imaginary family-mending play. Each example assumes a slightly different inciting incident but the same central action:

- After the loss of one member, a family mends itself.
- When a hidden will is discovered, a family mends itself after a traumatic loss.
- Because an estranged daughter returns, a family mends itself after a traumatic loss.

See if the inciting event that you've identified, and the central action of the play fit together in a way that is accurate and interesting to you. If so, you've probably found good material to work with as you use the next exercise to home in on the wants, needs, or desires that the inciting incident kindled. Note that when you consider your own character's role in the simple sentence you just created, you may or may not see your character as directly involved. They may even work against that action. The next exercise will aid you in any case.

Exercise 5.2: Inciting Incidents, Part Two

Here, we want to identify where a specific character fits into this inciting incident/central action which the final sentence from the previous exercise describes. Doing so will help to determine what desires drive your character through the play, or any character you analyze. First ask some questions—is your character central to the main action? Do they actively work against the story's main action? Do they pursue their own agenda in a way that neither directly helps nor actively seeks to obstruct the main action?

If your character actively participates in the action you've identified as central, the inciting incident you also found is probably their own. If, however, they pursue another agenda or begin participating in the central action later in the play, then another event set them on their current trajectory. So, you now want to answer new questions—"what was my character's personal inciting incident? What event set them on the trajectory they are on when they enter the story's action?"

For any character, we'll work to simply write the character's action and inciting incident in a statement expressed from your character's point of view. Again, this may incorporate the inciting incident you identified earlier, but many characters work against the central action of the play's protagonists or otherwise pursue their own desires. If that is the case for your character, see if you can simply state the action they are pursuing through the play as you did for the central action above a different way. If your character's central action is the same as the central action from the previous exercise, it may look something like this:

- In this play I struggle to overcome bias in my field.
- In this play, I mend my family after our traumatic loss.
- In this play, I work with others to birth a new era.

If your character works against the central action of the protagonist's or otherwise pursues their own agenda, it may look more like this:

- In this play, I struggle to maintain the status quo.
- In this play, I push my family out of my life so I can be free of my traumatic memories.

- In this play, I keep my head down and my family safe through all this change.

Whether you participate in the central action or not, take a moment to consider what your own inciting incident is, and whether yours is the same as the one you identified in the previous exercise. Examples include:

Same Incident and Same Action

- When an estranged daughter returns, I mend our family.

Same Incident, Different Action

- When an estranged daughter returns, I push her away so I can be free of my traumatic memories.

Different Incident, Same Action

- When I hear that my sister finally came home after all these years, I also go home to mend our family.

Different Incident, Different Action

- When I heard my girlfriend wanted to go home after all these years, I tried to shield her from her family instead.

This process of refining should leave you with a statement of what your character wants to do and what moved them to do so. Some event has upset their equilibrium and set them on a new trajectory. Now, they want something new or have a dormant desire awakened within them; that need drives them through the play. That need also implies actions that the character will need to undertake in order to fulfill their needs. In other words, you've discovered your character's *task* in this play.

As we move forward, keep in mind how the task is impacted not only by class privilege (the focus of this chapter) but also by the intersectionality of the character's identity. You may need to return to the standpoint chapter to refresh your memory on the social groups that your character resides in. For the moment, let's consider the impact of class privilege on a character's tasks.

Class and Character

As noted earlier, Americans don't talk about class and privilege. Karen Pittelman and Resource Generation argue "that privilege isn't something that can be turned on or off. While money can be laid aside unused, privilege is deeply embedded in our lives. It's a part of the experiences that make us who we are, that shape how we see the world and the way the world sees us." (221). Not acknowledging our privilege allows the divide between those with privilege and those without to grow further apart. Pittelman and Resource Generation go on to state, "Acknowledging how class privilege impacts our lives doesn't have to mean abandoning pride in ourselves. Our hard work is still hard work. Our fabulousness is still fabulous. It just means that, as young people with wealth, the history of where we are and how we got there is more complicated than a list of our merits" (221). We can be successful and still understand where we had the support of an alumni network, a phone call from a former boss, a supportive family member, family wealth, etc. to get us to where we are today. None of these diminish our accomplishments but acknowledging them works to undermine and dispel the centuries old myth that poor people are poor because they choose to be poor or are somehow "less" than those with wealth.

With self-reflection and a willingness to acknowledge privilege, we can see that hiding or not acknowledging privilege is one of many systemic power structures at work in our communities and world. An examination of where privilege comes from is important for us as well as for our characters.

Exercise 5.3: Check Your Privilege

This exercise allows you to think about your own class privilege. Remember to not be resistant to acknowledging your privilege. This is not a diminishment of your efforts, but instead an acknowledgement that where you are is not only by the fruits of your own labor. This sampling of questions from "Deep Thoughts About Class Privilege" (Pittelman and Resource Generation) homes in on key ideas to check our privilege.

- Have you ever been in a situation where you knew the 'right' way to act because of your class privilege? Or the 'right' way to speak? Or where you got a joke or a reference to something that you understood because you had class privilege?
- Does having class privilege affect your current income and expenses? Do you have loans? Car payments? Mortgage payments? Do you have a financial safety net or family resources you can fall back on?
- Has having class privilege affected your education? How so? Has it had an effect on your choices about schools? About what to study?
- If you've had to deal with a major illness or injury, either your own or a family member's, did having class privilege have an impact on your choices about treatments and options?
- Has having class privilege played a role in your housing decisions? Has it affected where you've lived in the past? Where you live now? The way other people involved like brokers, realtors and landlords, treated you? Whether you rent or own? If you own, did it impact the way you paid for your home?
- Think about a big decision you've made recently. Were there ways that having class privilege factored into that decision?
- Has having class privilege ever affected the way you've been able to cope with a difficult or painful time in your life? How so?

As with the "I Am.../I Am Not" exercise, take time to reflect on these answers for yourself to see where privilege exists in your life. Understanding your own privilege will, once again, help you create a more fully realized world for your character to live in. This exercise can easily be done with a specific character as well.

Tasks/Supertask

Tasks

In some fashion or other, an inciting incident awakens a desire in a character, but this desire cannot be fulfilled in a single sweeping act. Instead, the character must take steps toward fulfilling that desire. So, a character's attempt to fulfill this large task is made up of many smaller tasks, each an attempt to realize their driving desire. The above exercise moved us toward defining the type of large task that will define a character's actions throughout the play. We'll revisit this kind of broad task later in the chapter, but for now, we will scale back to better understand the many smaller tasks that make up the action of the play.

Again, simply put, all tasks arise out of a character's need, want, desire, aim, or goal. When it comes to smaller scale tasks, these are usually the scaffolded steps taken toward a larger goal. They want something, they must act to fulfill that want, and so they have a task, something the character will do to fulfill that desire in part or in full. If they work, the actions taken to fulfill these tasks bring a character closer to their desires, make them better equipped to reach out for those desires, or otherwise help them overcome any obstacles between themselves and the fulfillment of their desires. Often the way forward is not completely clear, and the character will find unexpected tasks along the way. Sometimes, they will set themselves a task that will surprisingly take them further away from their ultimate goal.

Remember, tasks are a reaction to the circumstances as the character sees and experiences them. Therefore, tasks are response that makes sense from that character's particular point of view in that moment. Even if we see things quite differently from our own, outside perspectives, the character follows some inner logic of their own, believing their actions are best.

Because you are aware of all the events of a play, you can see whether or not the character succeeds in their task. That character, however, does not. Since the character can't see the future, pay no attention to whether the tasks succeed or fail for now. If a character finds they are short on money and want to save every penny, they may set about a task *to persuade their friends to pay for dinner*. Even though you, as the actor, know the persuasion doesn't work, your character still sets about the task to persuade their friends to cover the meal as if it may. This distinction between what the actor knows and what the character knows means the character does not *try to persuade*, they simply *persuade their friends* in the full conviction that their persuasive skills could work.

Distinguishing between "trying to do" and "doing" may seem like it reveals very little difference. However, when it comes to an actor performing a task, there is a big difference between trying to put effort into an action without much conviction that it will succeed and genuinely doing the action as if it will. At every moment, a character is pursuing some task in the full hope that it will fulfill some desire that they have or at least get them closer to fulfilling it.

Stanislavski outlined several signs to look for when identifying and naming tasks. We have pulled three key signs for our purposes here and they include: tasks should be appropriate to the world of the play, tasks should be appropriate to the character, and tasks should be creatively stimulating. This applies to tasks Stanislavski categorized as essentially physical and ones that were more psychological (145–46). Asking whether or not a given task meets these standards will aid in keeping characters rooted in their own reality as well as relatable to the audience. As performers, asking if the tasks also excite your creativity will help you determine whether those tasks will keep you invested and anchored in that imagined reality as you perform.

Through the work earlier chapters, you've developed a strong sense of the character's circumstances and who they are within those circumstances. You should have a stronger sense of what fits within that character's world and what doesn't. That includes desires and their corresponding tasks. This sense of appropriateness is particularly valuable when you are looking at characters who lead lives unlike your own because of differences in their time, place, economic class, cultural background, or a myriad of other factors that make their lives unlike your own.

Since most characters diverge from you in at least one of these important ways, it is always important to check your assumptions about your world while you explore theirs. It is very easy to superimpose our own ideals and desires onto someone else by assuming that they are more or less just like us whatever our differences might be. This universalizing impulse would gloss over all the nuances that make people's lives distinctly their own. The same goes for the characters you encounter in a play. When you ask whether or not a task is appropriate to the character and to their world, you make space for diverse perspectives to emerge.

This may sound limiting when you are also making sure that a given task should excite your artistic interest. However, these limitations needn't take away from your creativity so much as channel it. Limitations like *appropriateness to the world of the play* give you bounds and direction which can spark your creative energies while focusing that creativity on things that help the whole play cohere. Knowing that your character is unlikely to set about a task of direct confrontation allows you funnel all your creative energies toward exploring evasive and oblique tasks that get the character what they want from a different angle. If the world of the play suggests that altruism is in short supply, you can direct your creative energies toward answering "what is behind these self-interested desires?" In the process, you may discover tasks that excite your imagination, and thus, keep you engaged with the imaginary circumstances.

For our purposes, we will seek tasks that are:

- Framed as positive action. *I want to do something* rather than *I want not to do something* or *I want to be something.*
- Appropriate to the character given their intersectional identities.
- Appropriate to the world of play.
- Exciting to your creative imagination.

If the tasks you identify meet these criteria, they should help you identify what drives the character through the action of the play and keep your creative faculties engaged.

Exercise 5.4: What's Needed on this Journey?

Consider what you have determined to be the overarching task so far, the task that defines the character's journey following the inciting incident. That task is probably no simple thing. Rather, it requires steps that the character must take to get them closer and closer all throughout the play. You can help yourself identify these smaller tasks by asking from the character's perspective "what do I need first?"

Take a look at the events of the play, bearing in mind your character's desires, and ask a few questions:

- What are the obstacles I'll face along the way?
- What do I need that I don't have?
- What do I need to do that I haven't done?

Identifying what your character currently lacks as well as what they need to overcome will help you quickly find the smaller tasks that act as the stepping stones to fulfilling their overarching desire. Knowing that your character has an obstacle helps you see that they must set a task to circumvent or overcome that obstacle. Knowing that your character doesn't have or hasn't done what they need to do to reach their goals tells you what tasks they'll need to set for themselves in order to put them in a position to reach it. Finally, bear in mind that a character's social class may open doors for them or help them circumvent obstacles. They may have access to opportunities or knowledge that someone from another social class simply doesn't have access to.

Tasks and Actions

Tasks suggest actions, but they don't necessarily define every action that a character takes as they try to fulfill that task. Rather, tasks may indicate an overall plan for fulfilling a need or a want, a collection of related actions aimed at getting them what they want. A series of actions that could be grouped together to form a strategy. If, for instance, a character wants to persuade another character to adopt their point of view or join their side in an argument, they may frame that task as "I want to convince them that I'm right." In such a case, the family of actions used to fulfill this task might include *reason* with them, carefully *explain* my ideas, and *lay out* examples that support my point. These actions comprise an overall strategy in fulfilling the task that could be defined as cerebral or intellect focused.

A character may, however, try to achieve a similar goal with different tactics. Let's say, for example, that they set themselves the task "I want to *sway* them over to my side." Phrased in this way, the task suggests that the character will more intentionally incorporate emotions into their strategy. Associated actions here could include *expose* the depth of my feeling, *express* my passion, and to *inspire* them to take my side. The strategy here is decidedly more of an emotional appeal, so it won't rely on intellect alone. It suggests that even if the character is going to incorporate reasoning and argumentation, those tactics will carry an emotional force in their execution.

If you are deducing a character's specific strategy in a moment like this hypothetical one, consider the clues that the script gives you. Look, for example, at the word choices and the structure of the lines, asking whether they suggest a particular strategy is shaping a given task. The words a character chooses to use are a window into their thoughts.

Consider appropriateness to the character, too. Does the character have a pattern in their behavior that suggests a favored mode of behaving in the world? Is the character using tactics that they are accustomed to? Is the character working inside the frame of social expectations for their identity? Are the circumstances desperate enough that the character is trying a strategy they wouldn't normally attempt? In short, what is most appropriate or "in character" for them?

Finally, consider appropriateness to the world of the play. Does the world of the play encourage or discourage specific behaviors in your character? Are they restricted by certain social norms and expectations of, for example, their gender? Are they coming from a position of class privilege in which many options are available to them as they pursue what they want? In this way, you can suit the strategy to the play you've constructed through the script analysis you've done so far.

Actions and tasks are deeply interconnected. We'll explore this connection more specifically in Chapter 6, which focuses on action. For now, what's important to note is that characters set tasks, whether consciously or not, as an active response to a need or a want they feel. These tasks imply actions and should be phrased actively, but they don't always outline every individual action. They aren't emotional responses even though they may spark emotions. You wouldn't say that a character is going to get what they want by being angry, but anger might fuel a strategy for getting what they want. Finally, tasks are influenced by the character's particular point of view and by the circumstances that form their current context (time, place, culture, etc.).

Supertask

Now, we return to those tasks that are large enough to drive a character through the entirety of a play and indeed shape the trajectory of their whole life. Smaller tasks often fulfill urgent, immediate needs. A character may set about a task in the hopes of overcoming some obstacle or otherwise taking them another step on their journey. But where do those steps lead? What are they journeying toward? The inciting incident that put a character on their current path awakened some desire, provided an opportunity to realize that desire, or otherwise motivated them to take actions toward fulfilling a great need within themselves. They then orient smaller tasks and the resulting actions toward that great task, what Stanislavski called a "supertask."

For a character, their *supertask* gives them a beacon to strive toward through the action of the play. A supertask draws all other tasks together, directing those smaller tasks toward a common aim—fulfillment of the supertask itself. This overarching supertask often constitutes a life's goal, all the hopes and needs of the character condensed into a single organizing motivation (Stanislavski 307). Having a strong idea of what a character wants from life is necessary for an actor because this central motivation effectively colors their entire identity and the actions they will take throughout the play. This need is part of who they are. It is their reason for being. Determining a supertask, then, is fundamental in character analysis because so much else depends upon it.

Characters rarely state a supertask directly, so determining one requires you to piece together clues until the puzzle begins to take shape. Even though they do not overtly state a supertask, you'll find many clues in their words. Very often, actions are equally revealing. This means you'll need to consider *why* a character does what they do. What does this person or their social situation lack that their actions are meant to create? Do they have a view of what their life should be that they are trying to realize? Or perhaps they have a vision for the world that they are trying to bring into being for more than just themselves. Do they seek justice? Pleasure? Love? Community? Power?

There is no single "right answer" to be found in these questions. You could look at the same character as someone else, the same set of given circumstances, actions, and lines as them. But, you may still arrive at a very different conclusion about a character's motivations. The choice you make will be distinctly your own and shade your character uniquely as a result. That's not a problem as long as the ideas you've arrived at are rooted in the play, and therefore, appropriate to the character's world.

Exercise 5.5: The Supertask

Using a character that you are analyzing, answer these questions. No single answer will necessarily reveal the character's supertask, although it may. Rather, when taken all together these answers should combine to create a clearer image of the driving force of desire in this character's life. Once that image starts to come into focus, succinctly phrasing their supertask should be easier. Answer from the character's perspective:

- What brings you satisfaction or a sense of completion?
- What is missing from your world?
- Who are the people you value most and what do you value in those people?
- Who are examples of people who have it all or have something you lack?
- What do you hope to accomplish with your life?
- What do you regret not having done?
- What do you worry about?

Take some time and see how the answers to your questions interrelate. If your character thinks the world lacks security, values loyalty and predictability, and hopes to gain control over their circumstances in this life, those answers may all point to some underlying desire. If your character derives satisfaction from making others happy, regrets causing rifts in their friendships, and worries about loneliness, then those answers point toward something else.

Now, try phrasing your character's supertask as a simple, active sentence (avoiding "to be"). Phrase it from your character's point of view. Consider whether or not it is appropriate to the world of the play and the character. Finally, ask whether or not you find this supertask creatively exciting or provoking.

A Northstar

A character's desires orient them outside of themselves and into an engagement with the world. If a character is on a journey, needs are their guiding lights, their north star. They need something beyond their current circumstances, and that desire cannot be satisfied without setting out on a journey and doing something to fulfill that need, although like any journey, they must take it one step at a time. Needs and desires permeate a character's life, always tugging them in a direction even if the character is not fully cognizant of this almost gravitational pull. Without desire, characters would be static, so finding out what motivates a character to act is a matter of finding out what gives them dynamism.

Inevitably, that character's desires conflict with the desires of others. What one character wants is typically irreconcilable with the desires of at least one other, propelling them into conflict. Sometimes, characters even have the same desires but refuse one another's methods for getting it. As we will further explore in Chapter 6, many of the actions that a character takes are a matter of finding a way around the obstacles that another character presents.

In taking these actions, characters reveal more and more about themselves. Often, the actions the character takes go so far as to transform them in the process. The meek people pleaser finds that they have the strength to stand up for themselves. The uncompromising idealist softens enough to accept other perspectives. Because of the revelations and transformations involved, the way characters shape their lives around the fulfilment of their desire is a form of identity construction. So, these urgent needs and the actions that characters are willing to perform in order to fulfill these needs both reflect and shape the character's identity. In short, knowing what motivates a character uncovers a wealth of information about *who they are* and *who they will become.*

Further Reading

Hurst, Charles E. et al. "Class, Income, and Wealth." *Social Inequality: Forms, Causes, and Consequences*. London: Taylor & Francis, 2016.

Mantsios, Gregory. "Class in America—2006." *Race, Class, and Gender in the United States*, edited by S. Paula Rothenberg, New York: Macmillan, 2007.

Pittelman, Karen and Resource Generation. "Deep Thoughts about Class Privilege." *Readings for Diversity and Social Justice*, edited by Adams, et al., New York: Routledge, 2013, 221–225.

ResourceGeneration.org.

Rothenberg, Paula S. "The Social Construction of Difference: Race, Class, Gender, and Sexuality." *Race, Class, and Gender in the United States*, edited by S. Paula Rothenberg, New York: Macmillan, 2016.

Quick Definitions

Action: Steps taken in pursuit of a goal.

Class: Divisions of people based on perceived economic and/or social status.

Privilege: Special rights or unearned advantage.

Task: Both a desire and the implied actions which must be taken to realize that desire. Something that a character needs to do as a response to an identified want or need.

Supertask: An overarching desire that drives a character through the entire action of the play, akin to a life's desire.

Chapter 6
Critical Race Theory and Beats

This chapter explores individual actions that characters undertake to achieve their objective or supertasks. These smaller actions, or beats, are impacted by the race or ethnicity of our characters due to social and cultural expectations.

An Introduction to Actions

Here's a small play:

Min wants a peanut butter sandwich. She goes to the kitchen, asks her partner for some bread, and makes her meal. She eats it. The end.

Not much of a play in that. Yes, Min has a clear *task* (or objective), the importance of which we established in Chapter 5. But, there isn't much of the dramatic action we might normally expect from a play. In part, this is because nothing prevents Min from achieving her goal. As a result, there isn't much *action* at all. We can't learn much about Min if nothing tests her character, so to speak, so she also stays fairly undefined and we can only make assumptions about her.

Simply adding, *Min struggles to make a peanut butter sandwich* doesn't solve the problem either because the actions as written also lack specificity. Actions need to be specific and engaging to hold the audience's attention. They also need specificity if they are going to reveal anything about Min herself. In short, we should ask "how is this Min's struggle and no one else's?"

As written, the actions above are so general they are nearly meaningless. *To go* could mean a hundred methods of transiting from one point to another. *To make a sandwich* or *to eat it* don't have much specificity to them either. But, very often, the play's script provides very little to go on in stage directions. An actor must make considerable creative effort to flesh out the details on top of the frame given by the text.

Let's try again:

> *Min wants a peanut butter sandwich, but she is snuggled up reading in the comfy corner of the couch. Her couch is too comfortable and her apartment too cold. She nestles in, ignoring the hunger and pulls the book closer. Her hunger will not be denied, however, and in frustration, she slaps her book down and surveys the distance from couch to kitchen. She decides that she will need slippers and grudgingly stretches her legs out from under her blanket. She curses under her breath when she realizes she kicked them off so far away when she sat down.*
>
> *Slippers on, Min shuffles to the kitchen, clutching her blanket around her. She hunts in the cupboard until she finds a jar of peanut butter. She weighs a jar of grape jam and a jar of strawberry, deciding whether to use one. When she turns, she notices that Nadia has the last of the bread. She smilingly implores Nadia to consider her craving for a peanut butter sandwich. She assumes a pitiful posture to make Nadia laugh. Winning the bread, she hums a happy tune for Nadia's benefit as she methodically spreads the peanut butter over the bread to ensure total coverage. She relishes the first bite and, blowing a kiss over her shoulder, she shuffle-dances back to the couch to finish the rest. The end.*

Granted, this may not be a deeply compelling play either, but it is far more dynamic and specific. Min has the same clear objective. She has obstacles, each of them requiring an action to overcome. The obstacles may be internal, as in Min's conflicting desires to stay comfortable on the couch or her desire to keep Nadia happy. Other obstacles are external, the cold or Nadia herself. These obstacles and her actions to overcome those obstacles communicate something about both her circumstances and Min herself.

The cold of Min's apartment may suggest that she is unwilling or unable to heat it. Min's interaction with Nadia reveal both the circumstances of their relationship and who Min is within that relationship. Her actions with Nadia hint that she is playful, hoping Nadia will reward a silly performance by giving up the last of the bread. The way Min builds and eats the sandwich show her enjoyment of food. Taken all together, specific actions help to paint a clearer picture of Min.

Action is central to dramatic performance. Hopefully, the example above illustrates, in some small way, that we learn about characters by seeing what they do to get what they want or by seeing the way characters react to their circumstances. These actions along with the actions of other characters constitute the plot which is a series of interrelated actions—one flowing from another and escalating in urgency all the while. The themes and ideas of a play emerge through the unfolding of a story often expressed through the interaction of characters.

Analyzing a character requires attention to their actions for a number of reasons. Actions typically arise from desire (wants or needs) and so actions firstly reveal a character's inner drive. Grouping all the typical actions a characters takes constitutes the character's accustomed tactics for overcoming obstacles to that desire. As obstacles and needs intensify the actions will too, revealing something more about this character—qualities that don't emerge unless the character is put under serious pressure. Plays often prove to be a crucible for their characters in this sense, uncovering something hidden within by lighting a fire underneath, the heat of which may transform them.

In this chapter, we are connecting critical race theory with Stanislavski's beats or units of action. Isolating race and considering how it is a factor in performing a character is vital for a more inclusive pedagogy because if we avoid the idea that race shapes character and action, that easily leads us to universalizing all experiences as the same. Such universalizing, in turn, tends to assume that the experience of a white person is universal. It also means that white students are less likely to examine their own experience of race in a meaningful way. One's racial identity, for example, shapes their view of the world and the way the world views them.

This chapter operates in light of two familiar concepts of critical race theory. First, that race is a social construction and is, therefore, fluid over time and influenced by a particular cultural context. That is to say, people who share a common ancestry may share physical traits, but social forces ascribe qualities and attributes beyond these physical traits in the creation of racial categories. These categories still vastly affect the lived experience of people who appear to fit a given racial category, which is to say that just because our racial categories are social constructions does not mean they don't have real consequences for people's lives (Delgado & Stefancic 9). Gloria Ladson-Billings reminds us that "Biologists, geneticists, anthropologists, and sociologists all agree that race is not a scientific reality. Despite what we perceive as phenotypic differences, the scrutiny of a microscope or the sequencing of genes reveals no perceptible differences between what we call races" (38). And yet, despite the science, there are countless ways that race impacts our day-to-day lives in positive and negative respects "based on the categorical understanding of race" (Ladson-Billings 39).

The second concept is because the experience of race is particular to social context and connected to a specific history of oppression Black, Latinx, Asian, and Native American actors will have unique experiences of, for example, America. They, therefore, are likely to have insights into the experience of race in America that are unlike one another's and unlike white actors (Delgado & Stefancic 11). This does not, however, mean that our white students have no experience of race in America. In fact, students are very likely to have experienced whiteness without having realized or examined it. So, every student will have a unique perspective, and no one is exempt from the conversation.

In order to express something about the character (in analysis and certainly in performance), we also need to think about actions with specificity. If Min brusquely insisted that Nadia hand over the last of the bread rather than goofily begged for it, that conveys entirely different information about the status of their relationship not to mention Min herself. Even if the same words are used, "can I have that, please?" the way Min enacts the asking matters a great deal. So, moving forward this chapter will also encourage you to find nuance in actions and see how two different verbs can subtly or dramatically shade a moment.

Finally, *actions* can help draw a clearer picture of a character's *circumstances*. Our actions are shaped by personal history, cultural context, social expectations, and any number of other factors we've explored so far. In particular, this chapter considers the way that social constructions of race have profound impact on a character's actions. Other factors about a character's identity and the corresponding social expectations will dramatically shape their actions, especially when two factors intersect as in gender and race. Be mindful that, just because this chapter is focusing on race does not mean it is always the only marker of identity that impacts a character's actions.

Privilege

As will hopefully become clear over the course of this chapter, we are not suggesting that someone's appearance, ethnic heritage, or cultural background predispose them to a defined set of actions. Rather, we want to acknowledge the importance of these same factors in the overall web of influences that lead a character to take or not take a specific action. As a first step, it is helpful to acknowledge the ways that race and ethnicity influence you.

Some may read "acknowledge the ways that race and ethnicity influence you," and respond, "but race and ethnicity don't affect me." Often, those that hold this opinion are typically white and have experienced a privileged position that allows them not to think much about race. However, even if the effects are invisible to you, they still affect your experience of the world. In fact, we would suggest, as Peggy McIntosh does extensively in her essay "White Privilege: Unpacking the Invisible Knapsack," that the invisible experiences of whiteness are themselves experiences with profound effects. Privilege, and in particular white privilege here, is not a cash machine from which one makes simple withdrawals to purchase benefits. White privilege acts as something of a social lubricant, easing one's ability to operate in a society that implicitly prioritizes your experience over others. Kivisto and Croll go on to assert that social dominance theory "overlooked important aspects of whites' own agency. In other words, while whites are in a dominant position, little attention is actually devoted to whites themselves, particularly the activities that they engage in that serve to maintain the existing racial hierarchy" (53). Regardless of your racial or ethnic backgrounds, we encourage you to investigate the ways in which privilege or bias impacts your life, and ultimately, the lives of our characters.

> That doesn't mean that to be white is to have an easy life nor does it suggest that being white shields you from all struggles. But, it does mean, along with the

advantages white people receive as a result of systemic racism, being white allows a person the privilege to "not think about race." Compare that relative ease to what Ta-Nehisi Coates describes in *Between the World and Me*:

> It struck me that perhaps the defining feature of being drafted into the black race was the inescapable robbery of time, because the moments we spent readying the mask, or readying ourselves to accept half as much, could not be recovered. The robbery of time is not measured in lifespans but in the moments we lose. It is the last bottle of wine that you have just uncorked but do not have time to drink. It is the second kiss that you do not have time to share, before she walks out of your life. It is the raft of second chances for them, and twenty-three hour days for us. (90–91)

Small actions, done or not done, add up throughout the day. So, it is useful to think about one's experience of race or ethnicity in both things done and things not done, feelings had or not had, and experiences big and small. Doing so equips you to see the same factors operating for the characters you analyze and play, factors they may not be fully cognizant of themselves.

Social construction thesis "holds that race and races are products of social thought and relations. Not objective, inherent, or fixed, they correspond to no biological or genetic reality; rather, races are categories that society invents, manipulates, or retires when convenient. People with common origins share certain physical traits, of course, such as skin color, physique, and hair texture. But these constitute only an extremely small portion of their genetic endowment, are dwarfed by what we have in common, and have little or nothing to do with distinctly human, higher-order traits, such as personality, intelligence, and moral behavior" (Delgado & Stefancic 9). It is worth stressing that social constructions are, of course, tied to their social context. While this chapter focuses on race in the United States, the experience of race in the United States is neither universal in all parts of this country nor is it universal to the world. Be sure that you consider all the given circumstances that are at play.

If a character walks through a world that has assured them that they belong wherever they go, they don't necessarily make a conscious choice to behave according to that message. Nevertheless, they move differently, speak differently, behave differently simply because that message of belonging has been subconsciously absorbed. If the messages are not universally welcoming, then more radical changes will happen based on context and they are more likely to be conscious adjustments. So, it's important to know:

- In your character's cultural context, is there a privileged racial and/or ethnic category?
- Is there a way that your character's culture implicitly or explicitly creates a racial and/or ethnic hierarchy?
- How does your character identify racially? Ethnically?
- Does their society categorize them the same way?
- Are there prominent stereotypes of that group in their culture? Has the character felt any of those stereotypes directed at them?
- In what contexts does your character feel excluded or singled out because of race or ethnicity? How so?
- In what contexts does your character feel included because of race or ethnicity?
- What are the relevant views on race or ethnicity that your character holds either consciously or unconsciously?

Exercise 6.1: Inventory of Race and Ethnicity

This inventory can be written from the perspective of the character, but we are asking you to begin by examining your own racial and ethnic background. Write without concern for sharing what you generate, although you're welcome to if you wish. Try answering the following:

- How do you identify racially? Ethnically?
- Do others view you this way?
- Do you feel that your society has certain expectations for people who identify as you do?
- Are there contexts in which you feel like race or ethnicity plays a positive or negative role in your experience? Places you feel less welcome? More welcome?
- Are there contexts in which you feel the need to change your behavior because of your racial or ethnic identity?
- Once you finish, cool down as you learned in exercise 2.3.

Sometimes, we have a sense of the role race or ethnicity plays in our lives, but have yet to put it into words. Doing so can give more clarity to that experience. Let this inventory help you to answer similar questions for the characters you'll analyze.

Actions, Objectives, and Obstacles

Actions, the deliberate and non-mechanical kind that we'll focus on, spring from the collision of a character's needs and an obstacle keeping them from that need. In short, there is something that your character wants—even if they can't name it—and there is something in the way of that objective. The character, then, reacts to that collision with some action intended to get past that obstacle. These actions may not be explicitly stated in the script. They may be implied, or they may be created by the actor. So, it will be up to you to decide how the character that emerges from your analysis would try to circumvent an obstacle based on their current circumstances.

As mentioned earlier, obstacles may be internal or external. An internal obstacle could be *doubt*. Viktor is missing his ring and he is sure it has been stolen. His friend, Alex, most likely knows something about it, but it doesn't seem possible to Viktor that his friend stole it. Viktor would like to come right out and ask Alex, but if Viktor is wrong, then he could damage their friendship by offending him. So, Viktor chooses to *dance around the subject*, he *hints* at his suspicions, and he *wonders aloud* if Alex has any idea how his ring could have disappeared. In short, he reacts to the obstacle of his own doubt with an approach meant to satisfy that doubt one way or another.

Alternatively, *fear* could present a difficult internal obstacle for a character to overcome. Miriam is coming in for a job interview. She's very interested in this job, but afraid that she's underqualified, that she will stumble over her words in the interview, and that they will take one look at her and decide to go another way. So, outside the door, she *mutters positivity* in her head, she *breathes deeply* to calm her nerves, and she *straightens herself* into a posture that makes her feel powerful. Like Viktor, she combines a series of small actions into a strategy to help her overcome her fear.

As you might expect, these internal obstacles are often more difficult to identify (or even notice at all) when you are first introduced to a character because they live in the character's mind. Internal obstacles are important to identify because they can be character defining, recurring throughout the play to create a constant struggle for the character. Perhaps, in a play about Miriam, she is regularly afraid, or Viktor's play centers on his doubts. If these inner obstacles prevent the character from achieving their objective, then much of the play and the performance of that character will be defined by actions to overcome it. Identifying that inner obstacle could, therefore, yield a wealth of insight into the character.

Much easier to find, external obstacles range from physical barriers to living, breathing adversaries with their own objectives. In fact, most plays are fueled by dynamic struggle between a protagonist (or protagonists) seeking an objective and an antagonist (or antagonists) whose objectives are in direct conflict with the protagonist's own. The play itself unfolds as a series of actions taken in an effort to resolve this conflict one way or another.

Obstacles tend to proliferate as the action of the play builds. Solving one problem may cause three more to spring up, and more difficult ones at that. Miriam gets the job she worked so hard for, but now, she finds out that she has beaten out a friend who also applied for that job. Now, she not only has the stress of a new job, but the resentment from a friend who believes they are more qualified and that Miriam wouldn't have been hired if not for affirmative action. One obstacle has developed into many.

Obstacles can also combine and even coordinate to block a character from getting what they want as in one antagonist aligning with another against the protagonist. Almost certainly the obstacles will intensify as the play builds to a final climactic crisis, pushing a character to find new and even bolder actions.

Exercise 6.2: The Obstacles I Face

Take a moment to survey the terrain between your character and what they want in the play or what they want in a particular scene. Write out the answers to these questions.

What inner obstacles does your character face?

What external (non-human) obstacles does your character face?

Who are your character's personal antagonists?

How does the race or ethnicity of my character impact their choices?

What privileges or biases, based on the character's race or ethnicity, are present?

These obstacles become, in a sense, questions themselves. For each, you will need to answer: "how will my character try to get past this obstacle?" Some actions will work, but as we'll discuss, most actions get your character only part way to an objective, if they work at all.

Inner Actions, External Expressions

Not all actions are easy to see. Actions that happen, for example, as part of a mental process are typically invisible in our daily lives. If Viktor weighs and balances his doubts as he talks to Alex, we might not see that conversation. We cannot hear Miriam's internal pep talk. Nevertheless, these inner actions need outward expressions. Partly this is achieved because internal actions combine with external actions to form an overall strategy to overcome one obstacle. The mind and the body work together. It is also worth noting that in order for internal actions to read to an audience, there must be some external expression. This could be as simple as Viktor visibly weighing one word before choosing another as he speaks or Miriam bobbing her head along to the rhythm of her personal mantra.

Revealing Actions

Tasks, established in Chapter 5, are revealing in and of themselves. They tell you what drives the character, what the character lives for, what pulls them through the action of the play. The actions that a character takes in order to get what they want are equally revealing, if not more.

Say three different characters encounter a tall wall encircling their common objective. Each must get to the other side, but there is no universal first response of *how to do it* among them. The first begins to climb, the second tries to find something to crack it, and the third begins to walk the perimeter carefully searching the surface for a door. In some small way, each initial response to the challenge hints at who this character is. What is their first reaction? How do they envision their obstacle? How do they usually handle challenges? How desperate are they to get what they want? When the first approach fails, each subsequent effort reveals even more about the character. Do they believe so fervently in their approach that they simply try to intensify it? What tactics are they willing to try only when they are sure they can find no other way? Can they adapt?

Not only are the actions themselves important, but *when* the action is attempted matters, too. Think of the difference in personality between a character who will only seek assistance as a last resort and a character who quickly acknowledges their shortcomings and seeks to combine their abilities with someone else's. Some characters leap at the chance to show off their strength or skill, relying on it as a skeleton key for all problems. Other characters are more experimental with small actions and carefully tread around the problem, waiting for a solution to come to them.

If we think chronologically about events of a play, early actions tend to establish the character's typical behavior, or their modus operandi. This is particularly true if the characters perform the actions before any obstacles present much trouble to overcome. These early actions constitute the *customary strategy*, a collection of tactics that has worked for the character.

The character may not like who they are or the mask they show to the world, but they are who circumstances of the past have led them to be. Their standpoint has led them to conclude that this is how they must act in the world. Perhaps they begin the play as a meek people-pleaser, choosing actions that they think will keep them out of the way and ensure the happiness of others. Perhaps they are an arrogant bulldozer of a person, choosing actions that push them toward whatever end they aim for, no matter the impact on others. If it weren't for the events of the play, this who the character would always be. The actions taken in the typical behavior mode are so habitual that they are largely automatic responses for the character in most circumstances.

Then the inciting incident sets off the action of the play and the character must respond to those events with a *modified strategy*. It may be that the character maintains their usual tactics, but intensifies them. Such characters test the limits of their typical strategy, perhaps scaling them up to solve larger than usual problems. Instead of switching tactics altogether, they push their already established tactics further by asking, "How far can kindness get me?" Or, "Can I shut down all opposition through force?" This character might not change much, only intensify or reveal qualities that were present from the beginning.

Rather than intensify typical strategies, other characters modify the strategy in a completely different way. They may shift tactics entirely, adapting their point of view and their actions to better suit the new circumstances. For example, they may decide that kindness hasn't worked so they try seduction.

To reiterate, the modified strategy is an evolution of a character's typical strategy. This evolution is due to failed earlier attempts fail or intensified conflict. Viktor realizes he can't *dance around* the subject if he is going to solve his personal mystery, so he begins to *directly accuse* Alex. Miriam realizes that all the internal power posing she does will not keep her fears at bay, so she carries that posture throughout her day adding a voice that *commands* rather than *requests* things of her colleagues. If such changes do not work for Viktor or Miriam, then the strategy must evolve again and again until the characters meet with success or failure.

In short, actions convey information about a character. The actions they choose reveal their standpoint and hint at the circumstances that shape them. This information is all the clearer when you collect those actions together to discern the character's typical strategy, the approach they typically take toward achieving their aims. Many characters must modify that strategy over time. These changes are a reaction to their changing circumstances and may also indicate a shift in the way they now view the world. Even if the character's journey is relatively circular, they end up in the same place they began, the events of the play have altered the character's point of view, and therefore, their actions

Exercise 6.3: Shifting Strategies

Take a character that you are analyzing and consider them at the beginning of their journey in the play, and the end. Collect their actions together and consider them as an overall customary strategy, a set of related actions that the character habitually uses as part of their modus operandi. How would you describe their accustomed strategy at the beginning? You can arrive at this by looking at several actions they perform and seeing if a pattern emerges. If so, define a broad category for that pattern.

Now look at the end of the journey to see if the character's actions can be similarly categorized. How would you label their methods for achieving their objectives at this later point? What is their typical strategy? How has it evolved into a modified strategy? Compare the overall strategies of the character at these two different points and try to answer:

- How does the character operate differently at the first point compared to later? How has their strategy changed?
- What has prompted these changes?
- How do these changes reflect back on the character's sense of self and the world?

Strategies could shift multiple times, so it is worth asking these questions at any significant shift in the character's approach to obstacles. It is also useful to repeat this exercise over the course of a rehearsal period for a focused scene study.

Specificity

Remember Nadia and Min and the bread? Let's say that Nadia wants to leave the city; she's tired of her cold apartment, tired of the press of people around her, and has the possibility of an exciting job somewhere less crowded. Min wants to stay in the city so she can finish school; she doesn't want to leave her friends, her professors are amazing, and she loves the feeling of infinite possibility she gets in the city. Neither knows if they can sustain a long-distance relationship. Their desires conflict and are irreconcilable. The two argue about what to do.

If we were to look at a full scene of this argument we would benefit from a great deal more specificity about the action. The word "argue," while an accurate description of the action, is too general if we simply stretch it to cover the entirety of the scene. Which also means argue is too vague to fuel a performance, as generalized actions are themselves vague responses to the given circumstances. An overly general application of a word like "argue", when used to cover everything in the scene, papers over the moment-to-moment nuance of all the smaller actions that happen within the argument, robbing the scene and characters of anything that makes this argument unique.

While it is true that you may watch a game of soccer and see two teams *competing against one another* the whole time, it is the details that matter. The back and forth as players switch up tactics, the big plays, the desperate defenses, and the rallies are what captivate us and make each game unique. So, while it is true that Min and Nadia *argue*, it is useful to ask *how* do they argue? How have their backgrounds socialized them to behave in an argument? How do they play the game? In doing so, you're likely to find a number of tactical shifts as both characters change their actions in response to one another. Tracking these moment by moment shifts in action allows you to trace the dynamic of the argument itself.

Again, specificity is key to this process. If you don't paint much, you might look at an apple tree and think *brown trunk, green leaves, red apples*. If you were to try to paint that simple green and red on a brown trunk, chances are that it would be rather flat, not measuring up to the tree itself. That's because in an apple tree, there are far more than three colors. Some of these colors come as a result of the way light and shadow play over the tree's surface, helping you see dimension. Other colors are simply unexpected if you haven't looked closely enough to see the surprising yellows, blues, or purples throughout. What's more, you may not have considered that not all reds are the same. Are those apples crimson? Scarlet? Vermilion? A painter who is sensitive to such nuances in color is more capable of reproducing them.

Actors paint with actions. Being sensitive to the nuances between one action and another helps you to better reproduce them. The details are vital to expression. Being curious about why one verb is different from another, is not unlike being curious about why emerald green evokes something different from olive. This subtle shading of an action adds more dimension to a scene.

Let's say that in our imagined scene, one of the first things Nadia must do is *tell* Min, "I've been offered a job. It could be a really great opportunity, but it's far away." That action, *to tell* Min about the job offer, is simply too vague to yield much insight into the character or the circumstances. To simply *tell* someone information is also not likely to hold the interest of an actor, let alone an audience. Specific actions, on the other hand, convey more and spark an actor's imagination.

If telling Min, "I've been offered a job. It could be a really great opportunity, but it's far away," is going to convey more than the information itself, it will help to make a choice about *why* Nadia wants to tell Min about this job. Does she want to test Min's reaction and gauge her partner's openness to an opportunity in another city? Does she know Min has responded negatively to conflict in the past? If so, she may *test the waters* with this line, carefully speaking it detail by detail and watching Min's body language. Or is Nadia's priority to the job itself, not her relationship with Min. If so, Nadia may *declare* the facts, dropping them with a resolve that does not invite comment from Min. Perhaps she wants the job, but also wants Min to be happy for her, and Nadia *celebrates* the information while stressing that this is a "great opportunity" for her. Each of these choices expresses different information about Nadia's desires and the status of their relationship from Nadia's point of view, but they all convey much more than the simple action *to tell* would. This is how making a specific choice adds dimension to the scene.

So, shortly after this, when Min *asks* Nadia to stay, does she *beg* her? Does she *needle* her? Does she ask in a way that is more of a *command* than a request or does she *lure* Nadia in with her words? Perhaps all of these happen over the course of the scene, making the sequence important. the changes in Nadia's actions along with Min's desires cause shifts in Min's tactic shifts as well. If we've established that Min likes to make a joke of things when she can, winning Nadia over with her exaggerated play-acting, then it may be that she avoids direct actions, preferring to cover emotions with humor. So, in our imaginary play, when Min says, "You can't leave me!" this is not very likely to be a *threat* or a *command*. Those actions are too direct for the character we've established. If Min prefers to come at things sideways and with a smile, this line is more likely Min *performing desperation* with an aim at making Nadia laugh or an exaggerated *beg* for the same effect. We could even make the argument that this is a seductive *lure*, but if so, then it is shaded in Min's particular performative style. Even though these actions are performed in Min's exaggerated humor, the actions are not any less sincere. Rather, they may reveal deep emotional investment *and* a fear of expressing that emotion directly. The shifts in tactics is not based solely on the actor's preferences. Rather, the answer should emerge from deciding *what is suited to the character* and *what is suited to the character's current circumstances.*

As we have seen earlier, strategies must evolve as the circumstances around the character change. As the reality of Nadia's departure settles in, Min might feel more urgency in proportion to the growing certainty that her partner is drifting away. Then, actions that don't fit Min's sideways strategy are more likely to spring up as she becomes more direct in her attempts to keep Nadia with her—she *pleads* in earnest, *bargains* anything Nadia wants, or *delivers an ultimatum*. These tactical shifts come from the pressure in Min to change. The pressure that a character's desires assert on them regularly force new and even surprising action from the character.

A Note on the Logic of Action

When we write, as we did above, about the sequencing of actions in a cause and effect fashion, it is easy to get the impression that actions are logically chosen as reasoned responses to a stimulus. Stanislavski repeats a theme of logic and reason particularly when he writes about the flow of actions (311–319). It seems important to pause and note human beings are often illogical and irrational in their actions. This is particularly true when our current circumstances apply pressure on us.

Characters will work against their own self-interests without even realizing. Think of the boss who wants to motivate their employees and so *barks orders*, *insults* those who come up short of expectations, and generally create an environment of hostility and fear. This may work for some employees, but it may also foster resentment as the employees withhold their best work out of spite, doing just enough to stay out of the crosshairs. The boss has traded a short-term sense of command for better long-term work.

That imperious boss, the lover who holds on too tightly to their beloved only to push them further away, and the parent who so completely controls their child that they leave the child wholly unprepared for the world—they all work against their own interests without realizing they are doing so. They have reasons, but that doesn't mean their actions are well *reasoned*. Just like any other human, characters can be misguided or even thoughtless in their actions or their actions may be a response to social expectations of their race, class, gender, sexuality, or other identity. Understanding the rationale for the action is key to character analysis.

It is helpful to see actions as stemming from specific causes—most actions are reactions. Remember, however, that a chain of cause and effect is not necessarily a reasoned progression. In your analysis, actions should make sense to you in that you see what caused them and why a character's particular point of view leads them to react as they do. That does not mean those actions meet some external standard of reason.

Exercise 6.4: In the Circle and Out of the Circle Revisited

Identify a desire that your character has in a discreet scene. For this exercise, find a simple but important objective that involves another character—something that they want from another character that moves them toward their ultimate goal, not necessarily the supertask itself. Use that goal as the title of a blank page—I want..." or "I need... from the other character. Read the scene through once before going on.

Now, use the rest of the sheet to draw three concentric circles, like a target with a rather large bullseye, on the page. Here's an example, the titles will be explained in a moment:

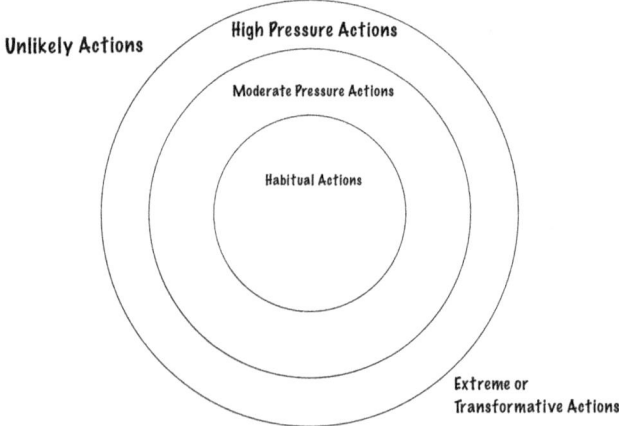

Figure 6.1 In the Circle and Out of the Circle Actions

Think of the innermost circle as containing actions that are customary for your character. These are the actions that your character usually takes to get what they want when they have not met with significant obstacles—think of the strategies you discovered in Exercise 6.3. Let's call these your character's "Habitual Actions."

Consider the next ring as a place for actions that are not so characteristic, actions the character would only attempt in the face of pressure. This ring will be for "Moderate Pressure Actions."

Meanwhile, the outermost ring is for actions that the character is willing to do in the face of intense pressure. The character may not even think of themselves as capable of these outer actions, but you know that it is within them to do these actions. These will be "High Pressure Actions."

There is also space outside the circles. This can be used for actions that occur to you, but that you don't believe the character would do under any circumstances—"Unlikely Actions." It could also hold actions that would suggest a total transformation has occurred in the character, the "Extreme or Transformative Actions." Try to use this space as little as possible, after all we are often surprised by what we are capable of in extreme circumstances.

Brainstorm as many actions that might be used to get your character's objective as you can think of on a separate sheet of paper. Write without considering whether these actions are likely yet, you can sort them soon.

Once you have your list, begin to sort actions to their appropriate circle. It is useful to reflect back on exercise 6.1 and how your character's racial and/or ethnic identities impact the range of actions available to them in the social or cultural conditions of the play. Bear in mind that the pressure of the character's circumstances can make many unexpected actions possible. Once you have this mapped out, you are better prepared to consider the flow of the scene and what actions your character will take within it, as we will do in a later exercise.

A couple of notes to consider:

- Actions taken at the beginning of the scene are not necessarily the least intense. The scene may well begin at a high intensity only to back off and ratchet up again.
- Your character may continue using actions from the center circle, even as the pressure is on. This map does not represent an outward progression from which there is no return. Rather, it is more of an accumulation of possibilities expanding when urgency builds.
- You may come up with actions that don't fit anywhere simply because they are misaligned with the pursuit of a particular objective. It's not, for example, a matter of pressure that Viktor doesn't do a silly dance to get information from Alex. The action simply doesn't fit that aim.

Beats of Action

Stanislavski's chapter, "Bits and Tasks" includes a vivid extended metaphor that likens the play to a turkey dinner which must be subdivided into smaller portions if it is to be consumed. Stanislavski explains that when analyzing a play, it is useful to have a method for subdividing the play into manageable pieces. Therefore, units of some kind must be devised. Rather than the all too large divisions of one scene and another or some other arbitrary division like pages, Stanislavski encourages divisions based on needs and actions. He proposes dividing a play into units he called *bits* (which evolved into *beats* in English). These *bits* or *beats* are measured by the length of time spent in pursuit of a particular objective called a *task* (139–143). A *beat*, then, contains all actions used in pursuit of that *task* and changes when either the character achieves their aim or modifies it as a result of some change in the circumstances. In short, a need arises creating a task that the character will attempt to fulfill through their actions, the unit of time spent acting in pursuit of that task constitutes the length of a bit or beat. Actions, then, are embedded within this unit as the character's response to the task.

In this construction, the small play of the peanut butter sandwich at the beginning of this chapter could be divided into four *beats*:

- Min going to the kitchen, defined by the need to get off the couch and into the kitchen and containing all actions that achieve that objective.
- Getting the bread from Nadia, defined by the need to get the last of the bread from Nadia and containing all actions that achieve that objective.
- Making the sandwich, defined by the need to actually make the sandwich and containing all actions that achieve that objective.
- Eating the sandwich, defined by the need to eat the sandwich and containing all actions that achieve that objective.

Stanislavski's method of divisions also allows a kind of telescoping between very small individual tasks/actions and very large units of action containing multiple smaller actions that all combine into the pursuit of one task. So, we could also look at the small play as one large unit:

- The beat of getting a peanut butter sandwich, defined by the need to satisfy a craving for said sandwich and containing all actions that achieve that objective.

In the above configuration, we consider all actions as unified under a single scene-defining goal. Alternatively, we could divide units even smaller than four by dividing the unit with Nadia and thereby more clearly see the way

Min balances the need for food with the need to make Nadia happy—employing different actions to serve those different ends. There are benefits to a wide focus and to a tight focus, no need to value one over the other. Rather, remember to use the scale that is most useful to you in the moment.

We will build out from this method of division in order to help you analyze a scene from your character's perspective. Doing so should bring into focus the dynamic shifts in actions/needs as your character responds to the obstacles they face. While this model can still scale up and down, we will focus units of action that are smaller than a single scene and usually larger than a single action.

Here's another small play in which Raimy wants to do well on an exam and has decided to study in the library with a small group of classmates. Each beat will contain multiple actions that are oriented toward a single objective.

- Beat 1: *Raimy wants to appear friendly*, so they enter the study area and warmly greet people by name. Raimy flashes a smile around the table and nods to Martin as Raimy sits down. Raimy cracks a joke about class before opening their notes to study in earnest. People start comparing notes, filling each other in on things they've missed.
- Beat 2: *Raimy needs a pen*. Celia makes a great connection and Raimy wants to write it down before forgetting, but Raimy's forgotten a pen. Raimy whispers a self-deprecating joke to Martin as a way of asking for a pen. Martin has a pen, but teases Raimy back instead of sharing it. Raimy doesn't mind the tease, but the classroom conversation is moving on. Martin is still in the mood for fun and continues to withhold the pen. After a few attempts, frustrated Raimy urges

Martin "Will you just give me the pen?" And Martin does so.
- Beat 3: *Raimy wants to make sure everything is good with Martin.* As the study session wraps up, Raimy checks in with Martin. Martin apologizes for going too far with the joke. Raimy reassures him that everything is fine and the two decide to meet up in the morning one more time before the exam.

All actions could be considered under the single task *I want to do well in school*, but breaking the mini-play down allows you to better see the character's attempt to balance small goals within that larger goal. As a result, you can see that doing well in school for Raimy isn't only a matter of studying, there is also a desire to connect to people. This means Raimy's actions aren't chosen solely to achieve one aim. This is similar to Min's balancing act between feeding herself and pleasing Nadia or Viktor's goal of getting his ring back while also maintaining a friendship with Alex. Negotiating multiple objectives creates its own kind of obstacle course when those objectives don't neatly align. Characters try to perform actions that satisfy multiple aims, if they can. If not, they will act to satisfy whatever goal has the highest priority for them in that moment.

Looking at beats of action in this detail also opens up the opportunity to factor in the way social constructions of race shape actions and decision-making. Again, this is not to say that people act differently because racial characteristics naturally correspond to particular actions. Rather, social constructions of race apply various kinds of pressure on people within that society, affecting their actions. For example, racial stereotypes that have been perpetuated in a society can make a person leery of fulfilling that stereotype or working outside of that expectation, depending on the situation. This pressure may shape their behavior in a way that deliberately avoids actions that may be used as confirmation of that stereotype by someone else.

Let's say that Raimy shows up at the study group and sees that they are the only Black student there. In the past, Raimy has been the only Black student in the class and felt an unspoken pressure to represent all Black people. This particular study group does not even need to do anything to consciously prompt such a feeling in Raimy. It's not fair to Raimy, but it happens anyway. Now, they feel the same pressure. When Martin teases Raimy about the pen in Beat 2, Raimy gets frustrated. But, unlike a white student in a similar situation, Raimy feels that if there is an expression of anger or frustration, they will confirm a negative racial stereotype amongst peers. So, a sudden tension emerges between a new beat and the new task—*I want to prove that stereotype wrong.* When Raimy comes to the line, "Will you just give me the pen?" the action could be a stern *demand*. Instead, in light of the new task, Raimy chooses a moderate tone and *rolls their eyes*, *laughing out* the line. The text of the line is the same, but the resulting action factors in Raimy's experience as a Black student feeling pressure to act in a particular way.

Again, Raimy's situation is unfair and things should be different. Raimy should be able to vent mild frustrations without worrying about whether doing so will have any further significance or repercussions. We should all work to diminish the enduring influence of racist stereotypes. Meanwhile, making room for these experiences in our analysis acknowledges their existence, and it is far easier to confront something if we acknowledge its existence.

Taking time to understand the impact of overt and less overt racism is imperative to understanding our characters. Microaggressions "are the small daily insults and indignities perpetrated against marginalized or oppressed people because of their affiliation with that marginalized or oppressed group" (Oluo 169). While that "one comment" about hair or dialect or skin color or clothing may seem small to the speaker, microaggressions have a cumulative effect on people of color. Microaggressions are "constant reminders that you are 'less than'" (Oluo 169).

Microaggression are important to take into consideration when discussing our character's actions. Characters of color who are subjected to daily reminders of their 'less than-ness" by dominant society may make choices in any given moment that respond to a level of exhaustion or rage toward a system that continually demeans and disenfranchises. While some actions may seem to "come out of nowhere", it is important to understand how race (and this includes whiteness) can be implicated in the rationale for a response that is seemingly over the top. Exploring the relationship between microaggressions and actions reveals that "seemingly unmotivated" actions are not unmotivated at all, but a direct response to an accumulation of negative actions.

Such pressures can become tremendously intense in particularly fraught moments, ones in which the legacy of racism in the United States quickly rises. Consider the much more extreme instance of a tense interaction of one driver with two white police officers. Whatever the intentions of those particular officers, history necessarily imposes itself on the scene meaning that a Black character will feel different pressure than a white character in the same scenario. No matter the weight of that pressure in any particular moment, we should consider the fact that ideas about race shape actions. Whether it *should* affect the scene or whether race *should* be a factor is beside the point. It does. It is.

Exercise 6.5: Mapping Beats

Copy a scene to study. Writing the text out by hand is great, especially if you are going to memorize it. Otherwise, a copy with wider margins than a typical script will do. Once it's copied, read it through. You'll write notes in the margins. Color-coding for clarity may help.

At the top of the scene, write out your character's super-task. Beneath that, write out the task for this particular scene; the smaller task should fit into a broader pursuit of your character's supertask.

Once that's done, identify the tasks that are internal to the scene. Identify these by identifying the obstacles that arise in this scene. Remember that subtle shifts can occur as one needs and another vies for priority. You may find a shift within a line.

Label each as a different beat. Title the beat with an active verb, something your character wants to do. Avoid the more passive "to be."

Now that you have beat, find the actions internal to those beats. When is each action attempted and for how long? When does the character shift tactics within that beat? Notice what prompts a change.

With this, you should have a sense of the flow of action in the scene. Consider multiple options for actions. Remember that a number of factors, including race, gender, and cultural context, may all exert pressure.

Throwing out the Map

With all this emphasis on charting out the flow of the scene, it is easy to forget that while a map seeks to capture terrain, it is not the same thing as that terrain. A map can't capture everything about the place it tries to describe, much less what experiencing that place will be like. So, with a map, you can make a plan, believing that you'll take a certain route, but you need to be flexible enough to adapt to information that the map was not able to tell you about. Your plan has to change.

Having a map and using it to make a plan in a scene operates similarly. It's useful to map a scene out so that you know a lot about what you can expect from it. It helps to have a plan for actions, it grounds you in the scene.

However, once you are experiencing the scene itself, you must be able to adjust to the experience. Implementing the plan lets you know what works and what must change when the plan meets reality. Having a map to begin with supports your ability to make such changes.

Further Reading

Coates, Ta-Nehisi. *Between the World and Me.* New York: One World, 2015.

Delgado, Richard and Jean Stefancic. *Critical Race Theory: An Introduction.* New York: NYU Press, 2012.

Kivisto, Peter and Paul R. Croll. *Race and Ethnicity: The Basics.* New York: Routledge, 2012.

Ladson-Billings, Gloria. "Critical Race Theory–What It Is Not!" *Handbook of Critical Race Theory in Education.* New York: Routledge, 2013.

McIntosh, Peggy "White Privilege: Unpacking the Invisible Knapsack." *Peace and Freedom*, July/August 1989.

Oluo, Ijeoma. "What Are Microaggressions?" *So You Want to Talk About Race.* New York: Seal Press, 2019.

Omi, Michael and Howard Winant. "Racial Formations." *Race, Class, and Gender in the United States.* edited by Paula S. Rothenberg, New York: Macmillan, 2016.

Quick Definitions

Beats (or Bits): Units of action taken in pursuit of something that the character wants, needs, or otherwise desires.

Ethnicity: A grouping of people based on shared national or cultural heritage.

Modus Operandi: The set of typical actions a character takes to get what they want.

Objective: A goal based on the character's desire, want, or need.

Obstacle: Those barriers, whether internal or external, that prevent a character from achieving their objective.

Race: A grouping of people based on similar physical or social qualities; socially constructed.

Strategy: A collection of tactics taken together toward the achievement of a goal.

Tactics: Discrete actions directed toward achieving a goal.

Task: Both a desire and the implied actions which must be taken to realize that desire. Something that a character needs to do as a response to an identified want or need.

Chapter 7

Disability Studies and Internal/External Adjustments

This chapter asks us to disrupt the expectation of able-bodiedness and/or neurotypicality unless otherwise noted. It unpacks how we can decenter "normalcy" in order to explore the full spectrum of physical and psychological processing for our characters.

Characterization

If you get the chance, find public places where you can do a little people watching from time to time. Find spots where people gather, where they pass by, where they can sit for a bit. The idea is to discretely observe in places where people are not performing for an audience. There, you simply observe with curiosity the way people carry themselves, their physical rhythms, and their gestures.

Notice the way some people lead from a very specific section of their body (the head, the chest, and the pelvis, for example). Try to sense the variety in personal rhythms and tempos. What are the gestures and attitudes that signal to you that someone is more closed off or open? This practice doesn't always have a goal. It is a simple reminder of the multitude of human variation, that there is no single "normal" physicality. This is a great moment to bring in the discussion of the social construction of disability. As disability scholar, Lennard J. Davis notes, "Focus not so much on the construction of disability as on the construction of normalcy. I do this because the 'problem' is not the person with disabilities; the problem is the way that normalcy is constructed to create the 'problem' of the disabled person" (1). As you are watching individuals move through space, recognize that way you are defining normal is just as socially constructed as what you consider abnormal. Davis goes on to argue that "One of the tasks for a developing consciousness of disability issues is the attempt, then to reverse the hegemony of the normal and to institute alternative ways of thinking about the abnormal" (12). The way someone physically expresses themselves is unique to them, the result of hundreds of small and large influences. Some of these influences are internally manifested and others are responses to the world around them.

At this point, you've gathered together a wealth of circumstances from which to construct your character and their world. Many of those circumstances have stamped themselves on the character's body, shaped the working of the character's mind, and produced a unique voice from them. Some of those circumstances have been with them since birth. Others have made their mark on the character as they grew up, developed interests, found role models, began careers, or otherwise began to enter their cultural context. All the while, they make adjustments to their behaviors, adapting to their social environment. We must be conscious that some physical manifestations of a character's circumstances, while deemed to be a "choice", are not. Much the same way, we talk about queerness as not being a "choice" and that there is a compulsory nature to heterosexuality—unless otherwise noted people are presumed to be "straight"—similarly, Robert McRuer argues "compulsory able-bodiedness functions by covering over, with the appearance of choice, a system in which there actually is no choice" (371). The presumption that a disabled body would ultimately and without question choose to be able-bodied negates the identity, power, and authority of the disabled body–relegating it to the abnormal and not-to-be considered. This chapter reminds us to think more holistically and inclusively about bodies and their function in the world of the play.

Here let's consider two dominant conceptual models of disability—the medical model and the social model. We refer to Joseph N. Straus's definitions. The medical model defines disability "as pathology, either a deficit or an excess with respect to some normative standard. Second, the pathology resides inside the individual body in a determinate, concrete location. Third, the goals of the enterprise are diagnosis and cure. If the pathology cannot be cured–if the abnormal condition cannot be normalized–then the defective body should be sequestered lest it contaminate or degrade the larger community" (462). The disabled body is an othered body, one to be gawked at, contained, isolated or repaired. On the other hand, the social model sees disability "as socially constructed rather than biologically given: the nature of disability, the kinds of conditions that are considered disabling, and the meanings attached to disability all vary with time, place, and context" (462). Thinking through how we see the bodies around us as well as the characters in the play through one lens or the other and how we privilege certain disabilities over others is important as we reflect on the lives and worlds of our characters.

A character may adopt physicality consciously or unconsciously. Susan Wendell argues, "Many other social factors can damage people's bodies in ways that are disabling in their environments, including (to mention just a few) tolerance of high-risk working conditions, abuse and neglect of children, low public safety standards, the degradation of the environment by contamination of air, water, and food, and the overwork, stress, and daily grinding deprivations of poverty" (482). There are a multitude of influences shaping a body and the way it moves. Perhaps the work the character does has rounded their shoulders or made them accustomed to speaking with calm clarity. Perhaps their privileged upbringing has meant years of elocution lessons and social pressure to display refinement. Maybe their personal rhythm is a reflection of the way their mind processes information and responds to the world. They may hold their body differently, for example, as a conscious response to cultural expectations that they perceive in the media. Alternatively, they may develop vocal habits as a way of signaling affiliation with a social group or as a result of the way their brain processes information without ever making a conscious decision to do so.

Now that you've identified the myriad sources of influence, we'll begin to look at how those influences manifest. Expressing those influences with adjustments to your body and voice is a process of *characterization*. By characterization, we mean adopting expressive patterns that are appropriate to the character rather than the actor. In this chapter, we'll connect the circumstances that you have gleaned about a character's life and the way those circumstances are embodied or vocalized. Remember that "multitude of human variation" will play an important part in this process, helping you to move away from generalized assumptions toward the important particulars that make each of us unique.

Observation

For actors, honing your observation skills helps you better see that there is material for characterization all around you, in the bodies of other people. Having a keen eye for the way people physicalize can provide you with inspiration for a character, so you don't need to pull a character from thin air. You can assemble them from observations you've made in the world. Grounded in observation, you can pull together physical behaviors, habits, and movements rooted in reality.

If you try to take in the entirety of a person's physicality all at once, you may find yourself quickly overwhelmed by how much there is to notice about even one body. When observing physicality, pay attention to small details, then notice how those details affect the whole body. These specifics provide anchor points in your observations and your future characterizations. Below are a few suggestions to help you focus your observations.

Leading from Body Centers

See if the person you're observing seems to lead from a particular part of the body, a center. Perhaps this section of the body is a center of attention for the person you are observing. Maybe it's a point of pride. Or, it could be an unconscious choice. Common leading points are the head, center of the chest, belly, and pelvis. Each point, as well as the degree to which it leads the rest of the body, changes the way that the rest of the body moves in response. They may also project a certain attitude toward the rest of the world.

Qualities of Movement or Physicality

The way someone gestures as they point out directions might be quick and sharp. They may cross a park in a sinuous glide. When you look at the movements of a person, see if you can assign a quality to that movement. Some observations might have to do with shape, line, and form as in "she walks in perfectly straight lines, holding her body in a way that feels very vertically symmetrical, and gestures in tight spirals." Other qualities you notice might best be expressed with metaphor as in "they have an expression like granite," or "his head's like a balloon trying to float away from his shoulders." You're trying to capture the quality of their physicality in a way that will make sense to you weeks later when the memory of that moment has faded.

Physical and Emotional Attitudes

The body of the person you are observing might suggest an emotional attitude or a physical posture toward their environment. You may notice this in the shape of the shoulders, the look in and movement of the eyes, or in the way the limbs swing. Certain physicalizations might suggest an open and comfortable attitude or a closed-off and even defensive one. They may suggest an inwardness of reflection, sadness, or a quiet and personal contentment. Some physicalizations suggest an outwardness that carries with it joy and positivity for all around or a frustrated anger with everyone nearby. Just remember that physical attitudes (like open, closed, high, low, wide, narrow) can freely mix and match with emotional attitudes.

Tension

Where do you see looseness or tension in the body of the person you are observing? You might notice someone has a lot of rigidity in certain parts of their body. Others might seem so loose that they appear partly liquid. Perhaps there's a specific part of the body that is much stiffer than everything around it, like painful joints. Notice the balance of tension and relaxation, observing the resulting physicality.

Rhythm and Tempo

You might notice that some people have a relatively steady rhythm. Whether fast or slow, there is an evenness to their actions. Others have a more syncopated or even erratic rhythm. Some people have a high velocity in everything that they do, others move at something more like a meander. How would you describe the overall rapidity of the person that you are observing? You may notice that the entire body is not unified here. Maybe they have a slow and steady rhythm in their pace, but their gestures slash out without warning. Remember, observe the physicality in all its particulars, then zoom out to see how everything fits together.

Exercise 7.1: Spying

Find a public place where you can quietly observe someone without being noticed. This is not an exercise in which you can simply substitute observing an actor in a movie or a video on the internet. Such practices aren't without value, but the goal here is to look for people who are not consciously performing for someone else.

Find three different people and make three different detailed observations about their physicality. For each one, take time to notice them in detail, and then notice how the details come together to make a whole. Observe quickly without feeling the need to make full and complete sentences. Make note of specific details from the categories above.

You may find that you have a hard time describing the movement with anything but a metaphor, as in "he walks like a duck." This is no problem, but after making that observation, try to explain what the metaphor means. How does someone walk like a duck? Is it the way they step? The way they bob their head? Is it something about attitude?

If you've come to this book as a designer or a director, you might also take a look at the broader picture around this person. Do the things they interact with or what they wear seem to project something about who they are? That may be good material for your design. Perhaps they are interacting with another person in a way that suggests something about the relationship between the two. Carefully watching the way people interact can help you direct actors as they explore the dynamic between their characters.

Self-Observation

When we practice observing others, that awareness often translates to self-reflection. Of course, we are not always able to make the fairest assessment of ourselves because we tend to bundle our self-observations with desires to be different in one way or another. It will be difficult to do, but it's important to separate observation and judgement, particularly when you observe yourself, and accept yourself as unique and worthy as an actor no matter what those things you wish you could change about yourself may be.

Then, observe with curiosity the way you move, the way you hold yourself, the shifts that occur as your attitude changes. Remember that the "pace of life is a factor in the social construction of disability" (Wendell 482). Pay special attention to what circumstances cause you to adjust your physicality. When do you need to perform extraordinary compulsory able-bodiedness even though it exhausts you? How are you different when you're cold and in an unfamiliar setting? What changes when you wake up with a lot of energy but nothing to do with it? Again, the point here is not to correct behaviors. The goal is to notice the way you physicalize in order to make adjustments to your physicality when you inhabit a character.

Physical Characterization

Your observations of others and yourself will yield raw material for *physical characterization*, the process of making adjustments to the way you move that are more suited to the character's physicality than your own. The changes you make may be subtle, though no less important. You may also need to make a series of large adjustments to appropriately modify your movements to reflect the character's circumstances. It is easy to assume that other bodies move more or less the same as yours unless the playwright has made explicit notes otherwise. Avoid the impulse to generalize, and instead embrace the diversity of human physicality by exploring how this character's body is unique.

When you are developing your physical characterization, you are creating a way of using your body that reflects a character's life and their circumstances. The adjustments you make should take into consideration their history, their culture, and anything that might have an impact on the way they move in their world. For that reason, there are limits to what observation alone can do. Often, you'll need some amount of research that can help you make suitable adjustments. Certain time periods and cultural contexts might have particular expectations and ideals for movement, not to mention fashion trends that significantly impact the way a character would or could move. Ask any actor who has worn a corset about how it changes physicality. In other instances, a character may have factors in their work, social life, or hobbies that have a physical impact on their movement. Here is a short list of possible factors for you to consider, each of which will have implications for your character's physicality:

Characterization Factors

- Age
- Physical ability
- Injuries
- Social context
- Cultural norms and expectations
- Interests, hobbies, or physical practices
- Occupation
- Habits
- Attitude and emotional state
- Present circumstances (time, place, and company)

As you think about how to adjust your physicality to the character's, taking the body all together, again, is simply too much. So, as you did when you observed others, find small details to adjust. Then, see how these changes affect the whole of the character. Think of your body as a deeply interconnected environment. The changes you make in one area will ripple out to change other parts of the body.

Exercise 7.2: Ten Things

Warm up to this exercise by writing out one way that each of the "Characterization Factors" listed in the previous section affects you. These may be small physical characteristics, or they may happen only in specific circumstances. Whatever the case may be, try to think about how these factors affect your body.

Then, for the rest of this exercise, use the character (or characters) that you have been analyzing all along. Looking at the "Characterization Factors" list again, try to determine at least one possible adjustment for each category. How is this character's physicality different from your own? What are the most important physical changes you must make? In the end, try to have a list of ten things. This may mean you have one factor for each category, but it's just as likely that you will find several important adjustments in only a few of the categories.

Note: This exercise should be repeated for the next two sections—Vocal Characterization and Psychological Characterization.

Vocal Characterization

Because it is a product of the body, the physical changes you make may alter your voice. Our focus up until now has been on adjustments to the body, but these deep connections often mean that voice and body can't really be considered in isolation. Many of the factors listed in the previous section will have unique implications for a character's voice. As before, some factors may require you to research what effects the circumstances have in the voice. Review the "Characterization Factors" list, but this time give special attention to the voice. A particular accent may stand out as the most obvious and complex vocal adjustment, but a voice accustomed to coordinating with other players across a soccer pitch or calming rowdy children may require an important adjustment, too.

As a start, you might consider listening closely to the voices around you. Try to listen attentively to the particular sounds one voice makes as opposed to another. Listen for the languid roundness of vowels in one speaker that may be absent in another. Listen for the crisp sharpness of a speaker's rapid-fire consonants. How does emotion alter the sounds of a voice? What about age? Do you hear someone alter their voice based on changes in their current circumstances, speaking differently depending on who is in the room? Perhaps this is something that you do yourself.

The body produces a unique voice depending on many factors that make a person's physicality unique to them. Present circumstances and personal history all play a part in crafting a person's unique instrument and the way they use it in the present moment. Now that you have a wealth of analysis bringing your character to light, physical and vocal characterization will be the most direct way that you express that analysis.

Psychological Characterization

We all process the information from the world around us differently. We also respond differently to it. Our neurological differences are as important to consider as any of the differences this text has touched on so far. Return to the "Characterization Factors" one more time and consider how this character's mind operates differently than your own. Remember that we are not assuming a normal or standard way that a character's mind *should* work, as if all other minds deviate from that norm. Once again, some factors may require research.

It's important to remember that some of the factors you discover here may seem invisible, as if they live only in the character's mind, and therefore, cannot be seen. Remember, the deep interconnection of the mind and the body means that what is happening in a character's mind will probably find some physical expression. It may be a repeated behavior, an expression, a pattern of pausing, or a particular way of reacting to stimuli. Part of an actor's artistic duty is to find external expressions for the internal life of a character.

Psychological characterization is a matter of reminding the actor that their way of perceiving and responding to the world is no more universal than their experience of gender, race, or class. It is an important consideration for you as you try to inhabit the character's particular point of view, then respond to the world as if that point of view were your own. Our neurological characteristics contribute to the ways we all experience the world differently.

Exercise 7.3: What if Café Revisited

Now that you have a new, deeper understanding of the circumstances that shape a character and the way that those circumstances shape physical expression, try returning to the "What If Café" exercise in Chapter 2.

Remember that this exercise can be done on paper or on its feet with other actors. Again, a director should consider doing the exercise both as a performer and outside the scene, giving suggestions to actors. Imagine yourself back at that café or set it up again. Give it multiple seating possibilities (chairs near people and separate, in corners and toward the center) and include a place to order.

Follow the simple directions at whatever pace feels appropriate—you will order at some point, you will take a seat while you wait for your order to arrive, and you will receive a text on your phone that will prompt you to leave before your order comes. Then, layer a few ifs from below on top of that skeletal frame, either enacting them or thinking them through and writing down possible behaviors and actions. This time, the questions should prompt physical and vocal adjustments from you. Again, let your focus be on actions and with minimal speaking overall. Let's try some different "ifs":

What if I was 75? What if I was 10? What if I was 47?

What if my arms had a more limited range of movement? Or my legs?

What if my personality was such that I prefer not to take up much space? Or sought contact with others?

What if I just received some wonderful news?

What if I am very lost and worried about it?

What if I work a very physically demanding job all day previous to this?

What if I feel keenly aware and even self-conscious of my body while I am in public?

What if crowds make me feel anxious and confined?

What if I am eagerly awaiting the arrival of someone I love?

As before, fill this exercise with your own suggestions. Stay attentive to physical and vocal shifts that the creative input of circumstances suggests to you. If you're working with others, be open to receiving ideas from others.

Ability and Characters

Our early assumptions about a character, particularly upon our first reading of the play, often get weighed down with the inherited cultural assumptions we bring with us. So, we tend to see a character based on certain expectations that have been transmitted to us through our culture. Doctors look like this. Politicians look like that. Athletes fit this mold. We think in types based on what we've seen before (usually in television and movies) and build our assumptions about character from that. Douglas C. Baynton reminds us that "Disability is everywhere in history, once you begin looking for it, but conspicuously absent in the histories we write. When historians do take note of disability, they usually treat it merely as personal tragedy or an insult to be deplored and a label to be denied, rather than as a cultural construct to be questioned and explored" (30). As we imagine our characters, we need to make sure that we are checking in with our own biases and cultural assumptions. Otherwise, we might assume that unless a script explicitly notes that a character uses a wheelchair to cross the stage, they don't. Playing into those cultural assumptions means when a character is in a wheelchair, we are more likely to assign it some symbolic or storytelling function. In turn, ability is rendered a metaphor (or a motivation, or an obstacle) on stage rather than simply a difference. Indeed, there's a reason for this. Historically, playwrights have used disability as a character's obstacle or as a thematic metaphor. That doesn't have to mean, however, that there is a certain physical norm we should expect from characters any more than there is a certain physical norm in life. As artists we can work to dismantle the biases and stereotypes surrounding disabled bodies if we incorporate a wider range of physical and mental abilities on our stages. This is necessary if our stages are going to reflect the physical and neurological diversity of our world.

Further Reading

Baynton, Douglas C. "Disability and the Justification of Inequality in American History." *The Disability Studies Reader*, edited by Lennard J. Davis, New York: Routledge, 2013, 17–33.

Davis, Lennard J. "Introduction: Normality, Power, and Culture." *The Disability Studies Reader*, edited by Lennard J. Davis, New York: Routledge, 2013, 1–14.

McRuer, Robert. "Compulsory Able-bodiedness and Queer/Disabled Existence." *The Disability Studies Reader*, edited by Lennard J. Davis, New York: Routledge, 2013, 369–378.

Straus, Joseph N. "Autism as Culture." *The Disability Studies Reader*, edited by Lennard J. Davis, New York: Routledge, 2013, 460–484.

Wendell, Susan. "The Social Construction of Disability." *Readings for Diversity and Social Justice*. edited by Adams, et al., New York: Routledge, 2013, 481–485.

Quick Definitions

Adjustments: The specific changes that an actor makes in order to represent a character unlike themselves.

Characterization: The process of making physical or psychological adjustments to one's typical expressions in order to perform a character's lived experience.

Disability: Impairment that interferes significantly with life activity.

Temporarily able-bodied: The understanding that everybody could become disabled by illness, injury, aging, etc.

Conclusion
Wrapping It Up

Some Final Thoughts

In many ways, the interdisciplinary nature of theatre is obvious—architecture, history, fashion, cultural and social customs etc. come together—however, we don't often reflect in the same way on acting technique or character analysis. This book is one step in engaging interdisciplinarily with our understanding of characters and their world, using theoretical conversations from across the academy. Our goal is to increase/encourage self-awareness among teachers, practitioners, students, and artists, and through that increased awareness, create a more vibrant character analysis, performance, or production. From an inclusive position, we can offer our characters a more diverse and fully realized spectrum of choices from which to engage in the world of the play.

Inclusive analysis requires vulnerability on our part as theatre artists. Whether you are a professor or teacher working through instruction, actors delving into characters, or designers working to imagine the physical and material elements of a script... all of us benefit from a certain amount of self-reflection and self-awareness when bringing the characters and world of the play to light.

While we split facets of identity apart chapter by chapter, for the purposes of identification in this book, it is crucial to think of these identity markers holistically and see how each aspect connects to the others. These elements are fundamentally interrelated. Each of these descriptors are part of a character's identity and how those identity factors come together lends itself to a discussion of intersectionality. Intersectionality came out of the Black feminist movement and was coined in 1989 by legal scholar, Kimberlé Crenshaw. She asserts, "the intersectional experience is greater than the sum of racism and sexism, any analysis that does not take intersectionality into account cannot sufficiently address the particular manner in which Black women are subordinated" (159). While Crenshaw's example is specific to race and gender, the intersectional approach is the landing point for this book. Reminding ourselves to consider how social and cultural identities of race, class, gender, privilege, ability impact our desires, our ability to empathize, our understanding of the other is imperative for our work as artists and as humans.

The actor's challenge is to identify with circumstances and character traits that are often outside of their own experience. Understanding the world of a play and the characters within that play requires theatre artists to inhabit the fiction as if it were their own reality. There are many paths one can take to performance, ours has followed a path forged through empathy and by engaging the identities often left in the wings.

Tying critical theory to techniques of character analysis provides a lens to see beyond the scope of our personal experiences. Discovering another point of view by learning, in detail, a character's circumstances, desires, and the actions they take broadens our sense of the differences around us even outside of the theatre. This is an exercise in strengthening empathy. In doing so, actors can perform stories that also broaden an audience's sense of difference, strengthening their empathy.

It's crucial that we acknowledge the diversity of human experience on the stage and in the classroom. There's a great deal of work to do toward inclusion in the theatre. There are diverse stories to tell, a variety of voices to bring into the creative process of staging a production, and actors in need of a wider variety of opportunity and representation. Our goal with this book is to shift and expand the focus of theatre artists toward diverse and underrepresented voices, to push the needle toward variegated influences. As we learn the craft of bringing a character to life, we need to see that there is space for all of us in that craft. We want this text to be a tool in creating that space.

Further Reading

African American Policy Forum (AAPF). "Intersectionality." www.aapf.org/2013/2013/01/intersectionality. Accessed 20 Sept. 2020.

Crenshaw, Kimberlé. "Demarginalizing the Intersection of Race and Sex: A Black Feminist Critique of Antidiscrimination Doctrine, Feminist Theory and Antiracist Politics." *University of Chicago Legal Forum*, vol. 1989, no. 1, pp. 139–167.

Matsuda, Mari J. "Beside My Sister, Facing the Enemy: Legal Theory Out of Coalition." *Stanford Law Review*, vol. 43, no. 6, 1991, pp. 1183–1192.

May, Vivian. *Pursuing Intersectionality, Unsettling Dominant Imaginaries*, New York: Routledge, 2015.

Romero, Mary. *Introducing Intersectionality*, Cambridge: Polity Press, 2017. ProQuest Ebook Central, https://ebookcentral.proquest.com/lib/stlawu/detail.action?docID=5166452.

Index

Italicized page numbers refer to figures in the text.

ability, characters and 173–174; *see also* disability studies
able-bodiedness 161, 162; temporarily 175; *see also* disability studies
action(s): beats of 152–158; in circle and out of circle revisited (exercise) *150*, 150–152; circumstances and 135; core relationship and 96–97; critical race theory and 131–135, 139–144; customary strategy 143; and decision-making 155; defined 129, 133; desire and, interconnectedness of 112; extreme/transformative 151; habitual 151; high pressure 151; inner, external expressions and 142; logic of 149–152; and microaggressions, relationship between 157; moderate pressure 151; modified strategy 143–144; obstacles 133, 139–142; overview (example) 131–133; privilege and 136–139; and race 135; revealing 142–144; shifting strategies (exercise) 145; with specificity 132–133, 135, 145–149; tasks and 124–126; tasks and, interconnectedness of 125–126; *see also* critical race theory; task(s)
action words 29–31
actor, character in 55–57
adjustments: defined 175; internal/external 161–174; *see also* characterization; disability studies
affect, defined 83
age 48, 76
Akhtar, Ayad 95
Altman, Irwin 68–69, 78
An Actor Prepares (Stanislavski) 8
antagonists 42, 45; defined 59
attitudes, physical and emotional 166
attraction 103–106; character analysis and 86–90; relationships and 85–86; understanding

(exercise) 87–90, 88;
see also gender; relationships; sex/sexuality

Baynton, Douglas C. 173–174
beats (bits) 153–155; of action 152–158; critical race theory and 131–159; defined 152, 159; mapping (exercise) 157–158; Stanislavski's conception 134, 152–158; *see also* action(s); critical race theory
Benedetti, Jean 8
Bengal Tiger at the Baghdad Zoo (Joseph) 110
Between the World and Me (Coates) 137
binary, defined 107
Black feminist movement (1989) 177
body centers, observation 165
Bornstein, Kate 90
brainstorming 151
Butler, Judith 86–87, 91

character analysis 2, 4, 5–10; approach 8–10; cooling down (exercise) 43–44; difficult empathy (exercise) 45–47; emotional inventory, beginning (exercise) 39–40; gender, sex, and attraction and 86–90, 106; "I Am," "I Am Not" statements (exercise) 36–39; overview 5–10; theoretical resources 8; *see also* class privilege; critical race theory; disability studies; gender theory and relationships; place attachment theory and given circumstances; reading tactics, script; standpoint theory

characterization: defined 175; disability studies 161–164; factors 169–170; physical 168–170; psychological 171–173; vocal 170–171; *see also* observation(s)
character list 13–14
character(s) 25; ability and 173–174; in actor 55–57; circumstances 61; class and 118–120; empathy for 40–44; gender, sex, and attraction and 86–90, 106; gender expressions and role playing (exercise) 100–101; identity of 2–3, 7; inciting incidents (exercise) 110–11, 114–118; (particular) point of view 5, 21, 41, 42, 81–82; supertask 126–128; tasks 112, 120–124; time and place impacts 75–77; *see also* class privilege
circumstances: actions and 135; *see also* given circumstances
cisgender, defined 107
class, defined 129
class privilege: check your privilege (exercise) 119–120; class and character 118–120; desire 112–118; inciting incidents (exercise) 110–111, 114–118; northstar 128–129; objective 112; overview 108–111; self-reflection 118; supertask 126–128; tasks 112, 120–124; tasks and actions 124–126
climax, defined 31
Coates, Ta-Nehisi 137
code words 18
Collins, Patricia Hill 38, 48

comparisons and contrasts, structure of lines 25–26
complex (multi-story) ifs 49, 50–51, 53; *see also* if(s), Stanislavski on
conflict 16
context: defined 83; place attachment theory and given circumstances 61–68
cooling down (exercise) 43–44
core relationship: and actions 96–97; competitive friends 102; defined 107; relationships as 92–97; role playing and 98; seismic shifts, changes in 94–96; specific dynamic for 101–106; *see also* relationships
Crenshaw, Kimberlé 177
critical race theory 2, 131–159; actions 131–135, 139–144; and beats 131–159; beats of action 152–158; implementing 177; inner actions, external expressions 142; logic of action 149–152; map 158–159; objectives 139–142; obstacles 139–142; privilege 136–139; shifting strategies (exercise) 145; specificity 145–149; *see also* action(s)
Croll, Paul R. 136
culture 76; dominant 78
curiosity, maintaining, script reading and 31
customary strategy 143

Davis, Lennard J. 161–162
decision-making, actions and 155
desire: and action, interconnectedness of 112; class privilege and 112–118; Stanislavski on 112; *see also* class privilege
details, discovering (exercise) 77–78
disability: construction of 161–162; defined 163, 175
disability studies 161–174; ability and characters 173–174; characterization 161–164; characterization factors 169–170; leading from body centers 165; medical model 163; observation 164–165; physical and emotional attitudes 166; physical characterization 168–170; psychological characterization 171–173; qualities of movement/physicality 165; rhythm and tempo 166–167; self-observation 167–168; social factors and 163–164; social model 163; spying (exercise) 167; tension 166; vocal characterization 170–171; what if café revisited (exercise) 172–173
Dolan, Jill 3
dominant culture 78; defined 83

emotional attitudes 166
emotional expression 30
emotional inventory (exercise) 39–40; "if, then" 54–55; "if, then" with characters 57
emotion(s) 51, 54; encouraging 54–55
empathy 33–36; antagonists 42, 45; character in the actor 55–57; for characters 40–44; defined 59; difficult (exercise) 45–47; feeling

35; "if, then" (exercise) 53, 54–55; "if, then" with characters (exercise) 57; ifs and 53–55; purpose 53; and understanding 47–48; *vs.* sympathy 34–35; *see also* standpoint theory; sympathy
essentialism, defined 59
ethnicity 48; defined 159; influences 136–137; inventory of (exercise) 138–139; *see also* race(s)/racism
exposition 15–16; defined 32
expression(s), external, inner actions and 142
external obstacles 133, 139, 140
extreme/transformative actions 151

facts, tracking (exercise) 72–73
fat studies 2
fear 140
femininity 99, 100; *see also* gender; gender theory and relationships

gender 48, 75, 76, 106, 177; character analysis and 86–90; defined 107; expectations (exercise) 99, 99–100; relationships and 85–86; as social construction 86, 90; understanding (exercise) 87–90, *88*; *see also* attraction; relationships; sex/sexuality
gender expression 87, *88*; character's (exercise) 100–101; gender expectations (exercise) 99, 99–100; role playing and 98–101
gender identity 87, *88*, 89–90

gender theory and relationships 2, 84–106; core relationship 91–93; core relationship and actions 96–97; gender, sex, and attraction and character analysis 86–90; gender expectations (exercise) 99, 99–100; language, clarifying 90–91; lines of attraction and repulsion 103–106, *104*, *105*; mapping relationship constellations (exercise) 92–93, *92–93*, 96; overview 84–86; role playing and gender expression 98–101; seismic shifts, changes in core relationships 94–96; specific dynamic for for core relationship 101–106
Gender Trouble: Feminism and the Subversion of Identity (Butler) 86
geographic locations 60, 75, 76; *see also* place attachment theory and given circumstances
given circumstances: defined 83; Stanislavski's conception 61–62; *see also* place attachment theory and given circumstances
glossary, generating 72; code words 18; familiar but uncertain words 18; new words 18; personal associations 18–19; script reading and 17–19; *see also* reading tactics, script
Gunderson, Lauren 56

habitual actions 151
Hansberry, Lorraine 13, 14
"Harlem" 13

hegemonic, defined 107
heteronormative, defined 107
high pressure actions 151
Hir (Mac) 95
home 60, 78
Hughes, Langston 13
hyperfeminine 99
hyper-masculine 99

"I Am"/"I Am Not" statements (exercise) 36–39; *see also* standpoint theory
identity(ies) 8, 75, 84; character's 2–3, 7; "I Am," "I Am Not" statements (exercise) 26–38; markers 176–177; relationships and 85–86; social constructions of 2; spectrum-oriented 90–91; *see also* social groups
"if, then" (exercise) 53, 54–55; with characters 57
if(s), Stanislavski on 33, 48–52; character in the actor 55–57; complex (multi-story) 49, 50–51, 53; defined 59; and empathy 53–55; "if, then" (exercise) 53, 54–55; "if, then" with characters (exercise) 57; simple (single-story) 49–50; what if café (exercise) 51–52, 171–173; *see also* standpoint theory
imagination, journey in (exercise) 62–68; after the journey 68–73; reactions and imagination, in detail 65–68; warm up 63–64
inciting incident(s) 16, 120; defined 32; exercise 110–11, 114–118
inclusive space 4

inclusivity 1
inner actions, external expressions and 142
Intemann, Kristin 48
internal obstacles 133, 139–140; fear 140; identifying 140
intersectionality 177, 178
inventory: emotional (exercise) 39–40; of race and ethnicity (exercise) 138–139
The Invisible Hand (Akhtar) 95

Joseph, Rajiv 110
journey in imagination (exercise) 62–68; after the journey 68–73; reactions and imagination, in detail 65–68; warm up 63–64

Kivisto, Peter J. 136
knowledge, privileged 42

Ladson-Billings, Gloria 134
language 11; clarifying, gender theory and 90–91; glossary, generating 17–19; revealing words 22–23; structure of lines 23–27; subtext 27–29; understanding, script reading 19–31; *see also* reading tactics, script;words
Lewicka, Maria 62
logic of action, critical race theory and 149–152; *see also* action(s)
Low, Setha M. 68–69, 78

Mac, Taylor 95
magic if 49, 59, 61
Mantsios, Gregory 109
mapping: beats (exercise) 157–158; relationship constellations (exercise) 92–93, 92–93, 96

masculinity 99, 100; *see also* gender; gender theory and relationships
McIntosh, Peggy 136
McKenzie, Marcia 76
McRuer, Robert 162
medical model, disability 163
microaggressions 156–157; and actions, relationship between 157
moderate pressure actions 151
modified strategy 143–144
modus operandi 143, 145; defined 159

neutrality 99
"no place like home" 60, 78
northstar 128–129
Nottage, Lynn 95

objective, defined 159
observation(s): from body centers 165; disability studies 164–165; physical and emotional attitudes 166; qualities of movement (physicality) 165; rhythm and tempo 166–167; self-observation 167–168; spying (exercise) 167; tension 166; *see also* characterization
obstacle(s): actions and 133, 139–142; critical race theory and 139–142; defined 159; exercise 141; external 133, 139, 140; internal 133, 139–140
openness 3
"operation licorice" 18

(particular) point of view, character's 5, 21, 41, 42; exercise 81–82
personal associations 18–19
physical attitudes 166
physical characterization 168–170
physicality (qualities of movement) 165
Pittelman, Karen 118
place: defined 83; dominant culture of 78; home 60; overview 60; time and 75–77; *see also* place attachment theory and given circumstances
place attachment theory and given circumstances 60–82; after the journey 68–73; associations 78; complexity of 60; context 61–68; discovering the details (exercise) 77–78; formative circumstances (questions) 74–75, 76–77, 79; home 60; imaginary circumstances 62–68; immediate circumstances 68; journey in imagination (exercise) 62–68; overview 60; past circumstances 68; present circumstances (questions) 74, 75–76, 79; questions 73; tracking facts (exercise) 72–73
play: re-reading 19, 31; script reading tactics 11–31; *see also* reading tactics
plot, elements of 15–16
point of view (particular), character's 5, 21, 41, 42; exercise 81–82
privilege: critical race theory and 136–139; defined 129; *see also* class privilege
psychological characterization 171–173
punctuation 23–24

qualities of movement (physicality) 165
queer theory 2
questions, place theory and given circumstances 73; formative circumstances 74–75, 76–77, 79; present circumstances 74, 75–76, 79

race(s)/racism 48, 75, 76, 133, 177; actions and 135; beats of action and 155–156; categorical understanding 134; defined 160; experience 135; influences 136–137, 156–157; inventory of (exercise) 138–139; microaggressions 156–157; social construction thesis 137–138, 155; stereotypes 155–156; systemic 137; in United States 135, 138; white privilege and 136–139; *see also* critical race theory; ethnicity
Raisin in the Sun (Hansberry) 13, 14; character list 14; opening lines 15; reading 13, 14, 15; title 13
reading tactics, script: action words 29–31; character list 13–14; curiosity, maintaining 31; elements of plot 15–16; glossary, generating 17–19; overview 11–12; personal glossary and 17–19; play, reading 16–19; stage directions 14–15; structure of play 23–27; subtext 27–29; title 12–13; understanding language 19–31; words, selection 21–22; *see also Raisin in the Sun* (Hansberry)

relationships 84; and actions 96–97; in circle and out of circle (exercise) 97, *150*, 150–152; as core relationship 92–97; defining 92–93; exploring 85; gender, sex, and attraction and 85–86; identity and 85–86; lines of attraction and repulsion 103–106, *104*, *105*; mapping relationship constellations (exercise) 92–93, *92–93*, 96; seismic shifts, changes in core relationships 94–96; specific dynamic for 101–106; *see also* attraction; gender; gender theory; sex/sexuality
repulsion 103–106
Resource Generation 118
rhythm, observation 166–167
rising actions 16; defined 32
role playing: character's (exercise) 100–101; core relationship and 98; defined 107; gender expectations (exercise) 99, 99–100; gender expression and 98–101

scene-defining goal 153
script: reading tactics 11–31; *see also* reading tactics
self-analysis 4
self-awareness 48, 176
self-inventory 87
self-observation 167–168
self-reflection 118, 167, 176
self-understanding 33
sequence, words 24–25
sex/sexuality 48, 75, 76, 106; character analysis and 86–90; defined 107; relationships and 85–86; understanding (exercise) 87–90, *88*; *see also* attraction; gender; relationships

silence 26
Silent Sky (Gunderson) 56
simple (single-story) ifs 49–50; *see also* if(s), Stanislavski on
social class 48
social construction(s): defined 107; gender as 86, 90; identities and 2; races/racism 137–138, 155; *see also* ethnicity; gender; race(s)/racism
social dominance theory 136
social groups 36; character's point of view and 41; "I Am," "I Am Not" statements (exercise) 38; standpoint theory and 38, 41, 48, 58; *see also* identity
social location 84, 85, 91; defined 59; standpoint theory 33, 36, 38, 39, 48, 58; *see also* place attachment theory and given circumstances
social model, disability 163
speaking 20; action words 29–31; *see also* language
specificity: actions with 132–133, 135, 145–149; critical race theory and 145–149; *see also* action(s)
spectrum, defined 107
spying (exercise) 167
stage directions 14–15
standpoint theory 33–58; antagonists 42; character in the actor 55–57; cooling down (exercise) 43–44; defined 59; difficult empathy (exercise) 45–47; emotional inventory, beginning (exercise) 39–40; empathy 33–36; empathy, and understanding 47–48; empathy for characters 40–44; history 36; "I Am," "I Am Not" statements (exercise) 36–39; "if, then" (exercise) 53, 54–55; "if, then" with characters (exercise) 57; if(s) 33, 48–52, 57–58; ifs and empathy 53–55; limitations 41; overview 33, 36; social groups 38, 41, 48, 58; socio-cultural context 58; sympathy 33–36

Stanislavski, Konstantin 8, 33, 122–123; beats (as units of action) 134, 152–158; desire and action, interconnectedness of 112; given circumstances with place attachment theory 61–62, 78–79; if(s) 33, 48–52, 57–58; ifs and empathy 53–55; *see also* action(s); critical race theory; place attachment theory and given circumstances; standpoint theory

stereotypes 9; races/racism 155–156
strategy(ies): customary strategy 143; defined 160; modified strategy 143–144; shifting (exercise) 145
Straus, Joseph N. 163
structure of lines 23–27; comparisons and contrasts 25–26; punctuation 23–24; sequence 24–25; silence 26; visualizing 26–27; *see also* words
subtext 27–29; defined 32; translations 28–29
supertask 126–128; defined 130

Sweat (Nottage) 95
sympathy 33–36; defined 59; *vs.* empathy 34–35; *see also* empathy
systemic racism 137; *see also* race(s)/racism

tactics, defined 160
task(s) 142, 152; and actions 124–126; class privilege and 112, 120–124; defined 130, 160; identifying and naming 121–123; supertask 126–128; "trying to do" *vs.* "doing" 121–122; *see also* action(s)
tempo, observation 166–167
temporarily able-bodied 175
tension, observation 166
theatre, interdisciplinary nature of 176
theatre classroom 2–3
theory 2; *see also specific entries*
Thomas, Jennifer 1–3
time and place: dominant culture of 78; impacts 75–77; *see also* place attachment theory and given circumstances
title 12–13
transformative actions 151
Tuck, Eve 76

understanding, empathy and 47–48; *see also* self-understanding
Undoing Gender (Butler) 91
United States 75, 109; races/racism in 135, 138

visualization, structure of lines 26–27
vocal characterization 170–171
Vrtis, Robert J. 3–5
vulnerability 3, 176; act of 2

Wendell, Susan 163
white privilege, racism and 136–139
"White Privilege: Unpacking the Invisible Knapsack" (McIntosh) 136
The Wizard of Oz 60, 62
words 11; into action 29–31; choice of 22–23; code words 18; familiar but uncertain 18; glossary, generating 17–19; new 18; patterns 23–27; personal associations 18–19; structure 23–27; subtext 27–29; understanding, script reading 19–31; *see also* language; reading tactics, script; structure of lines
Wylie, Alison 41

For Product Safety Concerns and Information please contact our EU representative GPSR@taylorandfrancis.com
Taylor & Francis Verlag GmbH, Kaufingerstraße 24, 80331 München, Germany

www.ingramcontent.com/pod-product-compliance
Lightning Source LLC
Chambersburg PA
CBHW052121300426
44116CB00010B/1750